The North American Third Edition

Cambridge Latin Course
Unit 1

Teacher's Manual

Revision Editor
Ed Phinney
Chair, Department of Classics & Director, University Foreign Language Center
University of Massachusetts at Amherst, U.S.A.

Consulting Editor
Patricia E. Bell
Teacher of Latin & Assistant Head of Languages
Centennial Collegiate and Vocational Insitute, Guelph, Ontario, Canada

Editorial Assistant
Barbara Romaine
Amherst, Massachusetts, U.S.A.

CAMBRIDGE
UNIVERSITY PRESS

Published by the Press Syndicate of the University of Cambridge
40 West 20th Street, New York, NY 10011-4211, USA

The Cambridge Latin Course was funded and developed by the University of Cambridge
School Classics Project and SCDC Publications, London, and is published with the
sponsorship of the School Curriculum Development Committee in London and the North
American Cambridge Classics Project.

This edition published 1988
Reprinted 1990, 1992

Printed in the United States of America

ISBN 0-521-34853-6 paperback

CREDITS
The Narrative Points and the plot summaries of the stories in the Stage Commentaries
were written expressly for this Manual by William D. Gleason, Latin Teacher at South
Hadley (Massachusetts) High School; the Grammatical Points and Sentence Patterns, with
Examples, were collected by Patricia E. Bell, Consulting Editor for the North American
Third Edition of the *CLC*.

Contents

Introduction

History of the Course in Britain and North America

The first edition of Unit I of the *Cambridge Latin Course* was published by the Cambridge University Press in 1970, and subsequent Units and Handbooks appeared in the years following; Unit V, the last in the series, was published in 1974. The *Cambridge Latin Course* (hereafter called the *CLC*) was innovative and attractive, and within a few years had been adopted by between a third and a half of the schools offering Latin in England and Wales. The *CLC*, though not formally advertised in the United States and Canada, was also adopted experimentally or formally by so many schools and colleges that by 1979, when planning for the second edition of the series was begun, a third of all sales of the *CLC* were in North America. (In 1976, for example, after three years of pilot tests in three Greater Vancouver secondary schools, the British Columbia (Canada) Ministry of Education had prescribed the *CLC* for all provincial schools offering Latin in British Columbia.) The early success of the *CLC* in North America was due largely to the widely appreciated visits of *CLC* officials and authors: in 1972, David J. Morton and E. Patricia Story, to a conference on innovative Latin textbooks sponsored by the Department of Classics at the University of Massachusetts at Amherst; in 1974, David J. Morton, to a workshop for Latin teachers at McArthur College of Education, Queen's University, Kingston, Ontario.

These British officials and authors were members of a committee, or task force, called the Cambridge School Classics Project, which had conceived, written, evaluated, and—with the cooperation of the Cambridge University Press—disseminated the *CLC* in Britain, in North America, and also in the Netherlands, Japan, South Africa, and in Commonwealth nations like Australia and New Zealand. The Cambridge School Classics Project (hereafter called the Classics Project or, simply, the Project) was first funded in 1966 by the Nuffield Foundation with a grant of £34,000, and with later grants by the same Foundation and the Schools Council. The Schools Council was a semi-autonomous educational body set up by the British government, based in London, working chiefly to develop and support new curricula and examinations in British schools. The Schools Council, by virtue of its support of the Classics Project, held copyright to the Project's publications, both the *CLC* and also materials for the study of Classical civilization such as the Foundation Courses, called *The Greek World* and *The Roman World*. When the Schools Council was dissolved, the copyright to publications of the Classics Project passed to the Schools Council's present successor, the School Curriculum Development Committee, which maintains offices at Newcombe House, 45 Notting Hill Gate, London.

The Classics Project originally comprised a Director, David J. Morton, then Lecturer in Education at the University of Nottingham, and two collaborating authors, Clarence Greig and John A. Jones. Their office was located above a store at 21 Silver Street, Cambridge, but was moved, in 1968, to its present location at 17 Panton Street, Cambridge. The office in the house at 17 Panton Street, owned by the Department of Education, University of Cambridge, is currently administered by E. Patricia Story, former Deputy (or—in American English— "Associate"), now Director of the Classics Project and Lecturer in the Department of Education, University of Cambridge. Maire Collins is Secretary for the Classics Project at this office, and Patricia Acres, Chief Editorial Assistant for the *CLC*. David Morton retired from the Directorship of the Project in 1987 (still remaining as Honorary Consultant) and was succeeded by Patricia Story.

In the late 1960's, when planning for the *CLC*, the Classics Project was influenced by the practice of more progressive teachers, particularly those who attempted, within the framework of traditional courses, to present their students with "Latin first"; this had been strongly advocated, in the 1950's and 1960's, by the handbooks for teachers which were written and distributed by Her Majesty's Inspectors. The Project also, reacting to the beginning of a disillusionment in structural linguistics, rejected the audiolingual methods (based on Skinnerian stimulus–response psychology) which had dominated the foreign-language teaching scene since World War II in both Britain and the United States; it preferred to structuralism a Chomskian approach in which rules of language were said to function, not only in single inflected words, but also across sentences and paragraphs. In the actualizing of Chomskian theory in the *CLC*, the Project was fortunate in the choice of its early consultant on linguistics, John Wilkins, who had a special talent for mediating the theories of Noam Chomsky to the Project's authors. As a result, the *CLC* aims to develop in students, by extensive practice in reading continuous Latin texts, a functional skill in reading which leads to the comprehension of Latin literature.

The Classics Project, however, when planning for the *CLC*, were also responding to requirements imposed by the educational situation in Britain. Comprehensive schools for all students were replacing the former double tier of "grammar schools" for the most capable students and "secondary modern" schools for the rest. Additional subjects were making the school curriculum fuller. In sum, if Latin teachers and their subject were to survive, they had to reassess their subject. Particularly, as their class periods were being reduced, they needed to reconsider the long-term value of time-consuming activities like English-Latin composition, and as they were increasingly forced to keep enrollments high by appealing to students who by themselves were barely motivated to enroll for Latin, they also needed to consider how they would capture and maintain the interest of young people who had little or no background in Latin or other Classics. The Classics Project responded to these educational needs by designing a Latin textbook series which teaches primarily, though not exclusively, the skills of reading and comprehension, integrates culture with language so that students can learn the social background in a minimum of time, and reaches out with dramatic devices to capture students' attention and interest from the very beginning and to keep it thereafter.

The Roman historical period which the Classics Project chose for illustration in the *CLC* was that of the early Empire. Their reason for this choice again reflected the contemporary need of teachers for topics which would capture and hold the interest of their students; for the early Empire seemed ideal for providing a historical background of topical interest. Its social and political structure was not only more colorful and widespread than that of the Republic, witness writers like Pliny and Tacitus, but also easier for students to understand and far easier for teachers—given the larger number of physical remains dating to the period of the Empire—to show in illustrations. Moreover, although the more readable poets, like Catullus, Vergil, and Ovid, dated to the period of the late Republic, Catullus' most interesting lyrics were about his personal life, and Vergil and Ovid reacted, each in his own way, to the establishment of the Empire by Augustus, the proto-Emperor.

The two original authors in the Classics Project, Clarence Greig and John A. Jones, devised the plots and wrote the Latin stories for almost all of Units I, II, and III. Suggestions for choice of characters and locales were gathered by a consultant on Classical civilization, Martin Forrest. When the Classics Project had largely polished the Stages (or "chapters") through Unit III, Stage 26, two additional writers, David C. Chandler and Robin M. Griffin, joined the Project. They, assisted by Dr. Pieter Seuren as linguistic adviser, helped write the remaining Stages of Unit III, 27–31, and select and adapt material from Latin authors for Units IV and V.

The Latin stories in the *CLC* have frequently been praised for their depth of characterization, realistic motivation, and sensitive reflection of the Roman social background, and there is no doubt that Clarence Greig was to a high degree responsible for these qualities. He was a Classicist of remarkable imagination with special talent for holding readers' attention while simultaneously teaching them, and his death in 1978 was a great loss to the Classics Project and to the Classics profession in general. But Greig's work has been carried on ably by Robin M. Griffin, present Revision Editor of the *CLC*, who has revised many of Greig's stories and written several new ones for the Second Edition of the *CLC*, especially for Unit IVA.

In the decade after the appearance of the *CLC*, the series attracted much experimentation and comment. College and University teachers who taught Latin to students who had begun with the *CLC*, commented positively on their ability in literary appreciation and criticism, less positively on their knowledge of the mechanics of grammar. The Classics Project, therefore, in cooperation with the Cambridge University Press, began planning, in 1979, a second edition of the *CLC* which would help students better integrate and consolidate their knowledge of grammar. They decided to level somewhat the steep gradient of implicit grammar in the stories of Unit III by simplifying and reorganizing the stories in old Stages 21–28, and by rewriting and adding stories to old Stages 29–31 (published in the North American Third Edition as Stages 35–40 of Unit 4). They also decided to add sections of explicit grammar (called "About the language"), more learning activities (called "Practising the language"), and a full section of exercises for reviewing word forms, rules, and sentence patterns (in a separate section called "Language Information"). Much of this master plan was drawn up by the Revision Editor, Robin M. Griffin, who then proceeded to implement it meticulously.

In 1980, David J. Morton and E. Patricia Story returned to the United States, this time with Rosemary Davidson, new Editorial Director, Schoolbooks, for the Cambridge University Press, to consult with American and Canadian teachers. These meetings were held in New England, in conjunction with the Institute of the American Classical League at the University of New Hampshire, Durham, and with the New England Latin Institute and Workshop at Tufts University, Medford, Massachusetts. As a result of these meetings, the Classics Project engaged Professor Ed Phinney, Chair of the Department of Classics, University of Massachusetts at Amherst (where the *CLC* had been adopted, in 1975, for classes in elementary and intermediate Latin), to rewrite the students' Language Information pamphlets or sections and the teachers' handbooks specifically to meet the needs of North American students and teachers, e.g. by using the American case order in paradigms of nouns, and by describing classroom procedure in terms used by North American teachers. The students' textbooks, the heart of the series, were to be compatible and sold on both sides of the Atlantic. This compatibility was rather difficult, if not impossible to achieve, though the Classics Project and Classics Editors from the Cambridge

University Press—first Ann le Neve Foster, then Elizabeth Bowden and Keith Rose—and Ed Phinney worked hard, with mixed success, to find English words and idioms which would be comprehensible in Britain, the United States, and Canada. The style of punctuation, however, and many of the analogies remained British. Unit I, in both the British and the North American Second Edition, was published by the Cambridge University Press in 1982, and the final textbook of the revised series, called Unit IVB, in 1988. The North American Second Edition is distributed in the United States by the American Branch of the Cambridge University Press; and in Canada, by the Irwin Publishing Company, Richmond Hill, Ontario.

The North American Second Edition of the *CLC* has won far more adoptions in the United States and Canada, at both the secondary and college level, than did the British First Edition. The reasons for the increased number of adoptions reflect partly the teachers' gratitude for the North American adaptation, partly the reduplication in the United States and Canada of the educational conditions which led to the formulation of the *CLC* in the beginning, viz. fewer hours for classroom instruction and more classes with students of very mixed ability. The inevitable result of this success, however, has been an increasing pressure from teachers for an entirely North American version, with American style of punctuation and North American analogies throughout, more attention to the context of the historical and social background (North American students are less familiar with the physical sites of the Roman empire than are British students.), and a format with hard covers, larger pages, and color illustrations which is more like that of other North American Latin textbooks.

A new committee has been formed, therefore, to prepare the North American Third Edition of the *CLC*. This new committee, called the North American Cambridge Classics Project (NACCP), includes among its officers Professor Ed Phinney as Director; Patricia Bell, Centennial Collegiate and Vocational Institute, Guelph, Ontario, Canada, as Publications Officer; and Barbara Romaine, Amherst, Massachusetts, as Editorial Assistant. These officers are supervising the writing of the North American Third Edition of the *CLC*; it comprises four hardbound students' textbooks, called Units 1, 2, 3, and 4, and accompanying Students' Workbooks and Teacher's Manuals. The Units in the North American Third Edition (1, 2, 3, and 4) are fully compatible with the Units in the North American Second Edition (I, IIA/IIB, IIIA/IIIB, and IVA/IVB).

Objectives of the Course

The Course has two major objectives:

1 To teach comprehension of the Latin language through practice in reading it:

2 To develop, through these readings, the students' understanding of the social and political history of the Romans, especially during the first century A.D.

The Course does not present the Latin language as an abstract linguistic system or merely as an exercise for developing mental discipline. Instead, it presents the language as the medium of the great culture and literature that molded it.

The Course attempts to present the subject matter in an intelligent and interesting way. There are two reasons for this. First, if students find the subject matter worth knowing, their chances of mastering the language increase greatly. Second, if students are interested in the subject matter, they are less inclined to treat the readings as routine exercises. Students eagerly follow the plot of a story, recognize and react to characters, and distinguish significant details in the socio-historical setting. In short, students take all their readings from the start as communicative sources.

Description of the Students' Textbook

The students' material is divided into four books, called **Units**. Each Unit is subdivided into chapters, called **Stages**, with the addition of a Language Information Section which contains a Review Grammar (In Units 2, 3, and 4, the Language Information Section also contains a Reference Grammar; in Unit 1 it is printed on the back endpaper.) and a Complete Vocabulary; a Guide to Characters and Places; Indexes of Cultural and Grammatical Topics; and a useful Time Chart. There are 48 stages in the four Units of the course: 12 stages in Unit 1; 8 stages in Unit 2; and 14 stages in each of Units 3 and 4.

Most stages begin with a number of pages on which new grammatical points are presented by means of **model sentences**, or in later stages, short model paragraphs, illustrated with line drawings. The model sentences are followed by several **reading passages** in which the new and old grammatical points are repeated. These narrative and dramatic passages are the core of each stage. They become longer and more complex as the course advances, but the choice of presentation and order are carefully controlled. Some passages are accompanied by English study questions which are also to be answered in English. Many of the earlier passages fit conveniently into a single class period; others require several periods. Below each passage are listed new words and phrases. In Unit 1, where most words and phrases are necessarily new, they are given in the form in which they occur in the passage and are translated in the sense required by the context. In later Units, they are also given in their basic form (e.g. nominative of nouns and adjectives, infinitive of verbs) and translated accordingly.

Each stage contains one or more **grammatical notes** dealing with a point of grammar which has been introduced previously or has appeared prominently in that particular stage. The grammatical note is usually placed late in the stage and is designed to be studied *after* some or all the passages in the stage have been read by the students. The grammatical note is *not* intended as an introduction to the reading material in the stage.

Next within each stage come the **grammatical drills**. Sometimes these drills provide practice in learning the new grammatical points, but more often they review old ones. The drills are done entirely in Latin or by translation from Latin into English. None of them require translation from English into Latin.

Near the end of each stage is an English section providing cultural **background material**. It focuses on a single feature of Roman civilization, usually one which has been prominent in the accompanying Latin passages. This background material, along with supplementary materials like slides, videotapes, wall charts, or reference books, will help the students understand Roman society and history. The teacher, depending on the ability of his or her students and upon the number and length of periods available, should devote as many periods as possible to presenting and discussing socio-historical topics. Total omission of these from the course will impoverish the education of the students and deprive them of an important reason for studying Latin: "What do the Romans have to say to us?".

A **Words and Phrases Checklist** is provided at the end of each stage for review of important common Latin words. Most words in the checklists have been met by students at least three times in their previous reading. Make sure that students can recognize and translate these words exactly as they appear, out of context, in the checklists. And emphasize these words in examination passages. When composing your own facsimile Latin passages for examinations, consult the Cumulated List of Checklist Words in Appendix A below, pp. 114–16, for the most important vocabulary on which students should be examined.

Words in the checklists are usually listed in the same way as they are in the Unit's complete vocabulary. The lists in Unit 1 give nouns in their nominative form and verbs in the 3rd person singular of their present tense. In later Units, as students become familiar with a broader range of inflections, they are presented with a different and fuller layout. Out of a total of some 700 words used in Unit 1, approximately 300 are included in the checklists at the end of the stages.

A **Word Search** is appended to the checklist in order to provide students practice in using Latin words to determine the meanings of English derivatives.

Inductive Teaching Method

Because the course presents grammar in a controlled context, students learn the grammar and vocabulary through reading passages and remembering particular instances rather than from memorizing charts and applying grammatical rules or vocabulary to readings. Ideally, the students themselves will derive general principles of grammar and groupings of vocabulary from the specific instances they remember from their readings, but do not assume that they will do this or leave them entirely to their own conclusions. If students do not themselves in the course of their readings consolidate grammatical rules and inflections, help them by eliciting the rule or inflection in question with appropriate questions. If students cannot answer, prompt them with examples of the rule or inflection taken from the previous passages. Often students, by remembering the context of the example, will translate it easily and thus be able to analyze it for order of words or inflections. If students seem at a loss, even when prompted, write the example on the blackboard, and if they are still at a loss, have them turn back in their book to the example. Often the context or an illustration will prompt them to remember the meaning of the example. *Only translate the example for them as a last resort.*

If, after establishing the meaning of an example (or several examples) a student still cannot get the pertinent grammatical point, ask leading questions. For example, if a student does not understand the contextual function of the dative inflection, prompt him or her with examples—say, from earlier in Stage 9, e.g. *Clēmēns hospitibus vīnum offerēbat.* If he or she cannot remember the meaning of the examples, write them on the blackboard or have the student turn to pp. 134–36 and read the model sentences (silently or aloud) and study the illustrations next to them. Then ask him or her to list (1) categories of verb meanings used in the context of the dative nouns, e.g. "showing (to)," "giving (to)," "performing (for)" etc., (2) the English prepositions which are used in each of the pertinent model sentences to translate the dative ending, e.g. "for," "to," and (3) the position of the dative nouns in relation to the nominatives and accusatives which frame them.

Obviously, the model sentences are particularly valuable as grammatical prompts because they are designed to illustrate a point clearly, in as few words as possible, and are vividly illustrated with a line drawing. Memorize these model sentences and their locations in the textbook so that you will be able to help students find them quickly.

Although the inductive method described above is very effective in helping students to consolidate rules or forms, sometimes time will not allow it. If so, simply refer students to the Index of Grammatical Topics (p. 225 of Unit 1) or to the Reference Grammar on the back endpapers (and in Units 2, 3 and 4, in the Language Information Section) and have students look up the rule or form and study it.

Avoid discussions about Latin grammar in the abstract, unless, of course, students initiate them. (Wide-ranging lectures on grammar often leave the majority of students, especially if they are young, confused or bored.) Encourage the students themselves to consolidate and organize their knowledge as they become comfortable with the material, helping them to articulate it correctly only when they have come to wrong or partially wrong conclusions.

Outline for Lesson Plans

A good lesson plan should specify five main activities, three of them primarily for helping students learn and organize new material: (1) meet, (2) comprehend, and (3) consolidate; two of them primarily for helping them reinforce what they have learned: (4) test their knowledge and (5) review. There follows an outline of a recommended lesson plan with suggestions for activities under each heading:

1 *Introduction*

Choice of activities by which students are introduced to a passage overall:
A Short preview of grammatical and/or cultural background
B Key comprehension questions to establish overall meaning of passage
C Grammar questions, if necessary, to establish meaning of difficult but crucial phrases or clauses

2 *Comprehension*

Choice of activities by which students' comprehension of a passage can be measured:
A Questions on content or deeper meaning and answers
B Reading Latin aloud with appropriate modulation, facial expression, and gestures
C Dramatization, in Latin or in English translation, as either a radio play on audiotape or a skit on videotape
D Line drawings, captioned with key words, phrases, or sentences
E Idiomatic paraphrase, e.g. TV/film script, or transcript of imaginary interview

F Extemporaneous retelling, in English, of a story to classmates
G Expansion as an English short story or one-act play
H Summary, in English, or—with older students—in Latin
I Translation into English

Comprehension questions and expressive reading are particularly suitable for helping students make their initial exploration of a passage's meaning, and are frequently used in class. Dramatizing, illustrating, paraphrasing, retelling, expanding, summarizing, and translating passages are better undertaken when the students are fairly sure of the meaning, and are frequently worked out by them in study hall or at home in preparation for the next class period.

The initiative for activities like comprehension questions or expressive reading aloud rests on the teacher; for the other activities, on the students. Nevertheless, as students become more comfortable with the material, some of them will be able, as a study hall or homework assignment, to prepare comprehension questions ahead or practice reading Latin aloud.

Comprehension questions should begin as questions about content or meaning, not about grammar. For example, ask questions like the following when the class is reading the first paragraph of "Fēlīx," Stage 6, p. 88, of the students' textbook:

What were the Pompeians doing?
What were they drinking? Where?
Were there many or few Pompeians in the inn?
What did Clemens do?
Whom did Clemens see? How did he greet him?
Fēlīx erat lībertus. What does *lībertus* mean?
What does this word tell us about Felix?

If students seem uncertain about the answers, take them again through each sentence slowly and locate the parts they do not understand.

Many of the exploratory activities suggested above, e.g. items 2A, B, D, and I, can be mixed to provide variety. For example, vary the comprehension activities for the first three paragraphs of a story as follows:

Paragraph 1, an easy one: teacher reads aloud; students explore meaning in pairs; teacher asks comprehension questions.

Paragraph 2: teacher reads aloud; students explore meaning individually; volunteers translate.

Paragraph 3, a difficult one: teacher reads aloud, pausing at intervals to ask the more proficient students for meaning of individual words; students explore individually; teacher asks comprehension questions;

students explore further in small groups, drawing illustrations or contributing to a group translation; the groups' "secretaries" show the best of their group's illustrations to the rest of the class, or recite, in turn, their group's corporate translation.

3 *Consolidation*

Choice of activities which prompt students to consolidate what they have learned:
A Spotting examples of an inflection, syntactic rule, or sentence pattern, and collecting them on the blackboard
B Questions for eliciting from students specific rules or forms, beginning always with concrete examples and moving on to abstract concepts
C Careful study of grammatical notes ("About the Language") and translation of sentence examples

For an example of a series of eliciting questions, see p. 10 above.

4 *Testing*

Choice of activities to test students' comprehension and retention:
A Aural-oral drills for a short period of 5–10 minutes

A story recently completed may serve as a starting point for reviewing either a single grammatical point or several of them. For example, use a sentence in the story as the basis of an oral substitution exercise. Focus on a line with a verb like *portābant*, and ask the class for the meaning of *portābant* and *portābat*, then *portāvērunt* and *portant*; then *portāvit* and *portant*; and finally for a translation of "they were carrying." The progression from easy examples to difficult ones should normally be gradual. Thus, in the example above, the person is varied first, but not the tense; then the tense, but not the person; and finally both variables are altered, and an English-to-Latin example added for more proficient students.

B Written quiz
C Diagnostic homework assignment, e.g. a written translation of a passage covered in class, or a page to be worked from the Workbook

5 *Review*

Choice of activities to reinforce what students have learned:
A Study of a grammatical drill ("Practicing the Language")
B Study of an exercise from the Review Grammar section and translation of sentence examples
C Vocabulary work

Review vocabulary from a story which the students have read and know well, emphasizing words which appear in the checklists. Ask students to close their books and tell you what they remember about the story, then ask them for the meanings of single Latin words in the story. If students cannot answer, prompt them by reading the phrase or clause in which the word appears or giving them an English derivative. You will find appropriate derivatives in the Word Searches at the end of each checklist (e.g. for Stage 1, on p. 18 of the students' textbook). Other sources for derivatives include *Webster's Third New International Dictionary* and *The American Heritage Dictionary of the English Language*. If the students know some French or Spanish, give them derivatives in these languages. Sources for Romance derivatives include *Petit Larousse Dictionnaire Encyclopédique* and *Breve Diccionario Etimológico de la Lengua Castellana*, 3rd edn by Juan Corominas (Madrid: Gredos, 1976). Teachers who own copies of the North American Second Edition Teacher's Manuals will find short compilations of English, French, and Spanish derivatives in Appendix A of each Manual.

Vocabulary work and review exercises in general are particularly appropriate at the beginning of a class because they can smooth the way for the learning of new material.

The Pompeian Setting of Unit 1

The reading passages in the students' textbooks are so written that they not only introduce and repeat grammatical points, but also integrate language and culture from the very beginning by incorporating as much authentic Roman subject matter as possible. The reading material is set firmly in a Roman framework and frequently introduces historical characters. Thus, Unit 1 is set in Pompeii, for the most part during the year immediately preceding its destruction, and focuses on the *familia* of the historical banker Caecilius Iucundus. Because the tragic fate of Pompeii is one of the best-known events in the history of the Roman empire, this Italian city, though small, is a very interesting entry point into the wide world of the Romans.

Presentation of Grammar

In Unit 1, students are introduced to basic sentence patterns, with both predicative and operative verbs. They learn verbs of all four conjugations and of some irregular ones in all persons of the present, and in the third person—singular and plural—of the imperfect and perfect indicative tenses. They learn the nominative, dative, and accusative inflections of nouns and adjectives—both singular and plural—of the first three declensions. They also learn how the Latin language shapes questions, and how it orders longer sentences with subordinate clauses headed by *postquam* and *quod*.

Concessions to the Limitation of Time

When the number of class periods is severely limited, remember the following guidelines:

1 Avoid spending too much time explaining every detail in the early stages.
2 Choose quite deliberately the stories in each stage which are to be read and studied intensively and those which are to be read more quickly or omitted altogether (see, for example, item 4 below).
3 Because study of Roman civilization is such an integral part of the course, leave some time for discussion of socio-historical topics even when time is severely limited. Choose one or two topics for fairly thorough presentation, although the history and fate of Pompeii would surely have high priority here (see background material in Stage 12, pp. 197–99, of the students' textbook).
4 Read the following passages quickly in class or omit them altogether. If you omit them, summarize them in English:

Stage 3 "in forō" and "tōnsor," pp. 34 and 36–37
Stage 4 exercise 2, p. 59
Stage 5 exercise 3, p. 77
Stage 6 exercise 1 ("avārus"), pp. 92–93
Stage 7 "post cēnam," p. 106
Stage 8 "pāstor et leō," p. 125
Stage 9 "in apodytēriō," p. 145
Stage 10 "statuae," pp. 158–59
Stage 11 "Lūcius Spurius Pompōniānus" (four scenes), pp. 174–76

A teacher who rushes through the stages will not cultivate in students a true proficiency in reading. Likewise, two or three class periods a week are probably not enough to assure proficiency; four periods a week should be the minimum. Ideally, periods should be spaced regularly throughout the week rather than crowded together. In particular, a double period is usually far less effective for learning than are two single periods on different days. Many schools follow a modular scheduling system, however, and teachers there have little or no control over the schedule of periods allotted them for Latin.

Time Allocation for Unit 1 in Junior and Senior High School

A suggested plan for teaching the entire course in high school, with suggestions for continuation in the Latin IV year, is as follows:

Latin I: Units 1 and 2
Latin II: Unit 3
Latin III: Unit 4
Latin IV: Further selections from Ovid's *Metamorphoses*; selected
             books from Virgil's *Aeneid* in the *Cambridge Latin Texts* series.

In the junior high school, the Latin I curriculum would be spread over two years:

Seventh Grade: Unit 1
Eighth Grade: Unit 2.

Remember that the grammatical gradient of the Course is spread over all four Units and that students have not completed their study of basic grammar until they have finished Units 1–4. This is important to remember because older Latin textbooks in North America attempted to set forth basic grammar in the first two books of their series, supposedly to be taught in two high school years or one college or university year. But aside from the reality that true learning always takes time, remember that a Latin curriculum, when rushed, leaves little time for anything except abstract grammar and arbitrary vocabulary lists, thus depriving students of the practice in reading cohesive Latin and of the thoughtful consideration of the socio-historical background which are the only sources of true reading proficiency in Latin.

At the high-school level, the authors recommended for continuation in Latin IV, after completion of the *Cambridge Latin Course*, are Ovid, in the *Metamorphoses*, and Vergil in the *Aeneid*. These authors are recommended because selections from their works typically appear on the Achievement Test in Latin, offered every June by the Admissions Testing Program of the College Board. This is taken by many high-school juniors or seniors who are studying Latin. In the *Cambridge Latin Texts* series, published by the Cambridge University Press, separate students' booklets and teachers' handbooks are available for Vergil's *Aeneid*, Books II (edited by C. H. Craddock), IV (edited by J. V. Muir), VI (edited by Anne Haward), and VIII (edited by C. H. Craddock). (Handbooks for *Aeneid* Books II, IV and VIII should be purchased from the Cambridge School Classics Project, 17 Panton Street, Cambridge CB2 1HL, England.)

Time Allocation for Unit 1 in College and University

A suggested plan for teaching the entire course in college or university is as follows:

Elementary Latin (Freshman Year):   Units 1, 2 and 3
Intermediate Latin (Sophomore Year): Unit 4 and selected readings
                                      from authors in the
                                      Cambridge Latin Texts series

Students will not have completed their study of basic Latin grammar until they have finished Units 1–4. The authors recommended for continuation, after completion of the *Cambridge Latin Course* in the second semester of Intermediate Latin, are more numerous than those recommended for high school Latin IV because college and university students do not normally take the College Board Latin Achievement Test. Among the authors recommended for continuation at the college and university level are those authors presented in adapted or abridged formats in Unit 4: Catullus, Vergil, Ovid, Tacitus, Pliny, Martial, and Suetonius. In the *Cambridge Latin Texts* series, published by the Cambridge University Press, separate students' booklets and teachers' handbooks are available for selections from Catullus (edited by R. O. A. M. Lyne), Pliny's *Letters* (edited by M. B. Fisher and M. R. Griffin), Tacitus' *Annals* II and III (edited by D. C. Chandler), Tacitus' *Agricola* (edited by D. E. Soulsby), and Tacitus' *Histories* (edited by P. V. Jones). Also recommended in the series is *Libellus: Selections from Horace, Martial, Ovid and Catullus* (edited by M. J. Tennick). (Handbooks for the Catullus, Pliny and Tacitus *Annals* should be purchased from the Project.)

Final Examination

At the end of each grading period or semester, the students' progress in attaining the grammatical and socio-historical objectives of the course should be measured with an examination. The Diagnostic Tests on pp. 110–13 below, although short and not designed as proficiency examinations, may serve as partial models. The following is an outline scheme for a true final examination:

1 Sight translation (30 points). The passage could be written by the teacher (who might emphasize the relevant checklist words listed in Appendix A, pp. 114–16 below), or it could be adapted from a story in one of the stages. The diagnostic tests on pp. 110–13 below could also be used or adapted, although they were written, as their name implies, to help students find their weak areas *before* taking the final examination.

2 Prepared translation (25 points). This passage would be taken from a story in one of the stages which the students had recently read or reviewed in class. Their understanding of the passage could be measured by their ability:
> to translate the passage into English,
> to answer in English comprehension questions about the passage (e.g. "When did the wolves enter the arena?"),
> to answer questions about the language (e.g. "Find an imperfect in lines 7–10."),

to answer questions on the historical or social references (e.g. "Why was Alexandria a suitable place for the young man in line 8 to study medicine?"),

to answer more searching questions about the subject matter (e.g. "What does this passage tell you about Aristo's personality?").

3 Grammatical analysis (25 points). Provide, say, a connected passage based on one of the stories recently read and leave blanks to fill in, preferably with multiple-choice listings of the correct form to be supplied along with several distracters beside each correct form (e.g. "Complete the blank ... *grātiās maximās agō* with the correct item among the following: *tū, tibi, or tē*.")

4 Socio-historical background (20 points). Ask students to write a short essay, answer short questions, or—particularly younger students—draw a map or diagram.

The practical difficulties of varying the outline above by including an oral examination should not discourage the teacher from attempting it, either on the final or on mid-year or mid-term examinations. Because, in an oral assessment of students' proficiency, correction and evaluation is instantaneous, an oral examination can help them more than a written assessment, which may take considerable time to grade. In such an oral examination, students could, for example, read aloud and answer questions on two short Latin passages, one prepared and the other at sight.

The increasing use of Apple //e's, IBM PC's or similar microcomputers in the schoolroom now makes possible instantaneous correction and other pertinent feedback for drills, quizzes, and examinations which have been programmed onto magnetic disks. Although the Course does not currently provide pre-programmed material for computers, this can easily be developed by both teacher and students with any of the popular authoring systems which have been designed expressly for foreign language teachers (e.g. PASSPORT, PROMPT, QUESTIONMASTER, or THE LINGUIST). All these authoring systems are available from Gessler Educational Software, 900 Broadway, New York City, NY 10003–1291 (telephone 212–673–3113).

Correlation of Unit 1 with American National Examinations

Many American and Canadian high school students take the Level I National Latin Exam (sponsored by the American Classical League and the National Junior Classical League) in early March of their Latin I school year. Since Latin I students using the course will normally have reached the middle of Unit 2 by March (ca. Stage 17), they will be quite prepared to succeed on the Level I exam. Because the exam caters to students using many different kinds of textbook, however, some of the questions will deal with elementary Classical mythology and history of the Roman Republic. If you wish, prepare the students for these questions by assigning them readings in widely available books like Edith Hamilton's *Mythology* and Chester G. Starr's *The Ancient Romans* or any available handbook of mythology and survey of Roman history and civilization. For further information about the National Latin Exam, back copies, and a syllabus, write to A.C.L./N.J.C.L. National Latin Exam, P.O. Box 95, Mt. Vernon, VA 22121.

Many American and Canadian high school students also take a Cambridge Latin Examination (sponsored by the North American Cambridge Classics Project) in the middle and at the end of their Latin I year. Examinations are based on an original passage of facsimile Latin which incorporates the basic grammar, vocabulary, and socio-historical background of each Unit, with questions in two parts, one testing comprehension and grammar; the other, socio-historical background. There are four different examinations, one to follow the conclusion of each of Units 1, 2, 3, and 4. A new set of four examinations is available to the teacher every year in June, and they may be administered at any time during the following school year. For more information about the Cambridge Latin Examination and back copies, write to the Resource Center, North American Cambridge Classics Project (NACCP), Box 932, Amherst, MA 01004–0932.

Audiocassette Recording for Unit 1/Slides and Filmstrip

Recording

Latin read aloud correctly is both a medium for expressing meaning and a joy to hear. The system adopted by the Course for its audiocassette recordings is the restored pronunciation, and the rules for pronouncing all letters of the Latin alphabet according to this system are summarized in Allen 131–32. If you are unsure about your ability to pronounce Latin according to the rules set forth in Allen's definitive work (see Bibliography, p. 121 below), listen to and carefully imitate the readings on the C–60 audiocassette which contains material from Units 1 and 2.

The following lively narratives from Unit 1 have been recorded by actors, and are often further enlivened with sound effects:

Stage	3	"vēnalīcius," p. 38
Stage	4	"in basilicā," pp. 55–6
Stage	5	"Poppaea," pp. 73–4
Stage	6	"Fēlīx et fūr," p. 90
Stage	9	"in palaestrā," p. 138

The text of the aural comprehension passage is as follows:

Metella et Melissa in urbe ambulābant. fēminae Quīntum cōnspexērunt. Quīntus in tabernā stābat et vīnum bibēbat. Metella erat īrāta. "tū es pestis," clāmāvit Metella. "Caecilius semper labōrat, sed tū nihil facis."

Metella et Melissa Caecilium quaerēbant. fēminae forum circumspectāvērunt. Caecilius nōn erat in forō. Metella ad tōnsōrem contendit. Caecilium nōn vīdit. Metella Melissam ad portum mīsit. Caecilius nōn erat in portū. Melissa ad Metellam revēnit. subitō fēminae Caecilium cōnspexērunt. Caecilius stābat prope theātrum. multī amīcī erant cum Caeciliō. poēta versum scurrīlem recitābat. Caecilius et amīcī poētam audiēbant et valdē rīdēbant. Metella nōn rīdēbat.

"ēheu!" inquit Metella, "fīlius meus nōn labōrat; sed rēs nōn est mīrābilis; pater quoque nōn labōrat."

Use this aural comprehension exercise at any point between Stages 7 and 12, depending on the age and ability of your students. Play a section of the recorded passage, press the pause key briefly to check (usually by asking comprehension questions) that students have understood what they heard, then release the pause key and continue with the next section. (Do not break the thread of the story by pausing too often.) If the students are quite proficient, play the entire passage through once or twice before questioning them.

Except for this special comprehension exercise, play the other recorded stories after your students have read them and feel comfortable with them. If students seem puzzled while listening, let them follow the text in their books. Audio recordings are missing the body language of the speakers and other contextual visual cues, and students who depend on these for understanding can be quite baffled by the meaning of an audio recording, even if they already know the story. Ours is the age of television, not radio!

Slides and Filmstrip

Because Unit 1 of the North American Third Edition has been so richly illustrated, no slides or filmstrip have been produced expressly for use with it. In the Stage Commentaries (pp. 20–104 below), however, references have been made to visual material produced for use with the

British First Edition and North American Second Edition for the convenience of teachers who own them. The reference "filmstrip" is to the *Cambridge Classical Filmstrip 1: Pompeii*, accompanying the Second Edition of the *Cambridge Latin Course*, and the number after it to the frame within the strip. Information about the frames within the strip is contained in a booklet distributed with the filmstrip. The reference "slide" is to the *Cambridge Latin Course Unit I Slides*, and the number after it to a particular slide. Information about the slides is contained in the First Edition *Unit I Teacher's Handbook*, pp. 29–35.

Stage Commentaries

STAGE 1: CAECILIUS

BRIEF OUTLINE

Reading passages } Caecilius, his house and household
Background material }

Chief grammatical point   word order in sentences with and without *est*

NARRATIVE POINTS

Date	*Setting*	*Characters Introduced*	*Story Line*
A.D.79	Pompeii: Caecilius' house	Lucius Caecilius Iucundus, wife Metella, son Quintus, slaves Clemens and Grumio, dog Cerberus	Cerberus steals food, and Grumio gets angry.

GRAMMATICAL POINTS

nominative singular: declensions 1, 2, 3
    e.g. *Clēmēns est in hortō.*
3rd person singular present: all conjugations (including *est*)
    e.g. *Metella in ātriō sedet.*
predicative adjective
    e.g. *coquus est īrātus.*
ablative singular in prepositional phrases
    e.g. *Cerberus est in viā.*

SENTENCE PATTERNS

NOM + *est* + predicate (N/ADJ)
    e.g. *Caecilius est pater.*
NOM + *est* + adverbial prepositional phrase
    e.g. *Caecilius est in tablīnō.*
NOM + adverbial prepositional phrase + v
    e.g. *pater in tablīnō scrībit.*

Model Sentences

Caecilius is working in his study, Clemens in the garden, Grumio in the kitchen; Metella is sitting in the atrium, and Quintus is enjoying a snack and a drink in the dining-room. Cerberus is sleeping on the sidewalk.

Many of the stories in Unit 1 are written around these characters, and students develop various attitudes, positive or negative, towards them. Do not force a "proper" interpretation upon them, but remind them, if necessary, of the historical context that does not allow the editors of the course to present, say, Metella working, like a modern woman executive, at the bank in the forum. Aside from being asked to maintain a fairly accurate historical perspective, however, the student should be allowed to see the characters in his or her own way.

Model sentences stand, as here, at the beginning of each stage and introduce new grammatical points. Sometimes these illustrate the formation of words, like the inflections of the plural in Stage 5 or the imperfect and perfect tenses in Stage 6. Sometimes they introduce a new sentence pattern, like *vīllam intrāvit* in Stage 7.

Your first step, when introducing the model sentences, is to set up the situation described in the sentences. Here are shown views of Caecilius, his *familia*, and the various rooms of his house in Pompeii. Include the picture on the title page in your discussion, although on the title page of Stage 1 Caecilius is shown in the forum, not in his house as on pp. 3 and 5.

Guide the class through the initial exploration of the model sentences. Read aloud the first model sentence or set of sentences in Latin; give students a few moments to make their own attempts to understand; then ask leading questions in English, using the accompanying picture as a guide. Couch the questions in concrete terms. For example:

coquus in culīnā labōrat.
Q. Who is in the picture?
A. The cook.
Q. Is he working or playing?
A. Working.
Q. Where?
A. In the kitchen.
Q. So what does the whole sentence mean?
A. "The cook is working in the kitchen."

Do not comment about the grammar in advance. Let the students discover the sense of a sentence for themselves, helped by both the narrative and visual context which generally give strong clues. Most of the students will grasp the grammatical point of a set of model sentences by the first or second example.

When the students understand a model sentence and can express its meaning in English, move on to the next one. Postpone any discussion of grammar until all the sentences have been read. Occasionally, before proceeding with questions about the next model sentence, ask a student or the class together to repeat in Latin the sentence you have just explored. But do not let the pace lag.

A second reading of the model sentences, in which the students read the Latin aloud and translate all or most of the sentences, is now in order. Take this opportunity to explore with the class some of the cultural features in the drawings.

Students will often comment on the new grammatical point and ask questions about it. If so, encourage them to suggest explanations for the new ending or other grammatical feature. Confirm their observations where correct, but do not expand the discussion until they have met more examples of the grammatical point in their subsequent reading.

Before or at the end of the stage, discuss and drill the new grammatical point with the students. Often a language note, titled "About the Language" in the students' textbook, can be used as the basis of the discussion. The note usually deals with a grammatical point introduced in the stories or model sentences of the stage read concurrently. Sometimes, however, a particular point is not discussed in a language note until examples of it have appeared for several stages. In such cases, the note has been postponed deliberately. It is recommended not to anticipate it, unless the students are quite proficient or mature.

While introducing the model sentences of Stage 1 to students who know little or no Latin, be ready for the following kinds of minor difficulty:

1 The lack of definite or indefinite article in Latin may confuse students at first. Help them select the article appropriate to the context.
2 *servus in hortō labōrat* (and similar sentences) is sometimes translated as "The slave is in the garden working." Do not label this translation as "wrong." Rather, ask students for other ways of expressing the Latin in English and guide them toward "the slave is working" or "the slave works." Students themselves will come to prefer these later versions.
3 Some common nouns, e.g. *coquus, amīcus*, are treated as names by some students, at least at first.
4 Prepositional phrases like *in ātriō* should be treated as whole units and not broken down into preposition and noun at this stage.

Cerberus

Grumio has fallen asleep after preparing an elaborate meal and is snoring. Cerberus enters and jumps onto the table. He is eating the meal, when he is startled and barks. Grumio wakes up and chases him out of the kitchen.

Illustrate the growling sound of the name "Cerberus" by vigorously rolling the "r"s, and similarly the "r" of *lātrat*. Praise the student who asks whether Cerberus was named after the mythological guard-dog of Hades. Refer students to the photograph, on p. 84 of their textbook, of the *cavē canem* mosaic in the vestibule of the House of the Tragic Poet in Pompeii. The threatening nature of the mosaic is perhaps to be explained by the fact that the two entrances on either side of the private vestibule where the mosaic was laid led to stores which attracted the public.

On the blackboard, draw a cartoon of Cerberus standing on the table, even if you can only draw a stick figure. (Students will develop a certain affection for otherwise capable teachers who show themselves human and less than perfect, at least in draughtsmanship.) When you draw the dog on the table, ask a student to read out the relevant Latin sentence, *canis in mēnsā stat*. Then students might go to the board and draw their own sentences on the board for others to identify. During the second reading, a group of students at the front of the room could act out the story, while those remaining in their seats could read the text in chorus. Younger students in junior high school, especially, enjoy and learn well from this kind of activity. Use the drawing and ground plan of a Pompeian house on pp. 14 and 15 of the textbook to provide visual referents for phrases like *in ātriō*, *in tablīnō*, and *in culīnā*.

Language Note

After students have studied the language note, they might translate further examples of sentences which you have composed to illustrate the language note's comments on word order. Avoid analyzing inflections. Focus attention on the sentence as a whole, not on the individual words.

Drills

Exercise 1   Type: completion
            Missing item: noun
            Test of accuracy: correct sense

Exercise 2   Type: completion
            Missing item: prepositional phrase
            Test of accuracy: correct sense

In many of the drills in this Unit, students are asked to choose from two grammatically correct answers. They should complete the blank with the answer-choice that makes the better sense.

The Background Material

Caecilius and his House

Our knowledge of Caecilius derives mainly from the important collection of business records on 153 waxed tablets discovered in 1875 by archaeologists in a strong-box, or *arca* in his house. The following itemization, translated from a tablet, indicates the range and diversity of his financial interests:

	sesterces
Loan	1,450
Sale of timber	1,985
Sale of land	35,270
Rent of fullery	1,652
Grazing land rented from the town council	2,675
Auction of linen on behalf of Egyptian merchant	[amount not stated; Caecilius' normal commission was 2%]

You will find translations of two tablets in full in Lewis & Reinhold II, 332–33; a translation of a letter by August Mau, the excavator who found the tables, in Marx 127–30; and selected Latin transcripts (mostly auction records and rent receipts), in Marx 42–49. For further references, see Bibliography, pp. 119–22 below.

Caecilius' house is Regio V, Insula I, number 26 on the archaeological grid-map printed in Maiuri, Brion, and the *Pompeii AD 79* Catalogue. The house was large and well furnished, but in its present condition is unexciting, apart from the lararium and the realistic bronze portrait bust, complete with wart on chin (original now in Naples Museum). Note photograph, on p. iv of the students' textbook, showing Caecilius' street, now called the Via del Vesuvio, with the door of his house at the right and the Vesuvius Gate at the end. Correlate this photograph with the plan of Pompeii on p. 43 of the textbook.

The bust (filmstrip 1; slide 1), once believed to portray Caecilius Iucundus himself, is now dated to the Augustan period and more plausibly regarded as a portrait of Lucius Caecilius Felix, an ancestor or perhaps actual father of Iucundus. The lararium was decorated with marble panels showing, in low-relief, scenes of the disastrous earthquake of A.D. 62, which left much of Pompeii in ruins. The first panel showed the Temple of Jupiter, the nearby Arch of Drusus and two equestrian statues about to collapse, an altar, and a bull being led to sacrifice (filmstrip 6; slide 6). The second panel showed the Vesuvius Gate, only a few yards from Caecilius' front door, on the point of collapsing. Unfortunately, both panels have been stolen, and are now accessible only in photographs.

The drawing and ground plan of a Pompeian house are printed in the textbook, pp. 14 and 15. They are simplified to show the basic components of the *domus urbāna*. In reality, the house of Caecilius was more elaborate than the house depicted. Once students have become familiar with the layout of a simple urban house, they may go on to study, interpret, or copy the plans of actual, sometimes more elaborate Pompeian houses. Plans may be found, for example, in Paoli 54–69, Brion, Maiuri, and Grant, *Cities* 111–38.

The topic of houses can be further illustrated with the photographs in the students' textbook on pp. 13, 16, 17, 29, 89, 93, 165; filmstrip frames 3, 4, 7, 8, 12; slides 3–14.

Metella

Although the character of Caecilius is based on an actual historical figure, Metella is entirely fictional. Do not tell the students, unless they specifically ask, that Metella was not real. By emphasizing her fictional nature, you may diminish the students' curiosity about her.

Metella is presented in the Latin stories as a matron, however, and the discussion after her name in the background material of Stage 1 focuses on the life of a typical Roman matron. On p. 5 of the students' textbook, Metella is pictured seated next to a table with a distaff and spindle, and pointing toward Clemens in the garden (to whom she is about to give an order). By the first century, the role of a wealthy matron in spinning is more likely to have been supervisory, but she may have done it herself on occasion, or taught some slaves.

For more information about women in ancient Rome, see Balsdon, *Roman Women*, Lefkowitz & Fant, and Paoli 113–9. Compare the relatively sympathetic presentations of these authors with that of Carcopino, ch. 4, who appears to have interpreted the vitriolic satires of women by Juvenal and Martial rather literally. The contrasting viewpoints, should you wish to present some of them to your students, might spark a stimulating discussion, particularly if you have any budding feminists among your students and do not object to controversy in your classroom!

Look up information about spinning, weaving, and the clothmaking industry of the Classical world in Book 2 of the Classical Studies series of the Cambridge School Classics Project (CSCP), *How the Greeks and Romans Made Cloth*.

For more information about the businesswoman Eumachia, see Will.

Suggestions for Discussion

1 The contrast between modern houses and the Pompeian *domus urbāna*. Besides the differences in layout, discuss reasons for the more inward-looking orientation of the Pompeian house. Consider also the means of running it: slaves, water supply, types of fuel and appliances for heating and lighting. Junior high school students might enjoy drawing a plan of their own house next to a plan of a Pompeian house,

then writing briefly about the differences, or explaining which one they would rather live in.

2 The different sources of our knowledge about Caecilius. "If our own civilization were destroyed, how could future archaeologists find out about how we lived?"

Words and Phrases Checklist

You will find on p. 12 suggestions for using these checklists as reviews of important vocabulary. When assigning the checklist for study at home, first review it orally with students, discuss derivatives where helpful ones exist, and—especially—remind them that, at home, they should cover the English translations with a piece of paper when they are checking themselves with the lists. Some students, of all ages, enjoy making small flashcards for the vocabulary words in the checklist: Latin word on one side of a card, English on the other, with perhaps a Latin contextual sentence and an illustrative or mnemonic drawing. The junior high or high school teacher may want to use similar, but larger flashcards in class. Their advantage, at home or in class, is that they can be shuffled like playing cards so that the next item is unpredictable, and students are less likely to sneak a look at the meaning, if this appears on the back of the card. Or the teacher may transfer the checklist to an overhead transparency and project on the screen wall, progressively uncovering with a sheet of opaque paper each successive meaning as a student recites it. The advantage of this review method is that visual reinforcement of a student's oral answer is provided immediately. Or the students may copy the words of the checklist into notebooks, writing the English meaning, then listing derivatives where they exist, along with definitions copied from dictionaries. The advantage of such a vocabulary notebook is that parents, who may be anxious about the merits of their children studying a "dead" language, are relieved to find out, when they look at the notebooks, that it has applications to contemporary English.

Several teachers of younger students, in our observation, keep flashcards with basic vocabulary words in a large treasure box, dubbed "Caecilius' bank-box." When several minutes remain in the period, the teacher may retrieve a flashcard, or "prize" card, at random. Should a student know the meaning of the Latin word, he or she might be rewarded with a more tangible treasure, a piece of candy or a cardboard "sesterce" coin that can be traded, along with future cardboard "sesterces," for larger prizes. Should a student not know the meaning of a bank-box word, he or she might be required to give up a previously earned "sesterce." (Each day, a student may be appointed "banker," or Caecilius-for-a-day.) Older students, of course, in collegiate institutes or colleges, can learn their basic vocabulary without enticements like the above but they should be quizzed periodically on checklist items so that they realize that they are being held accountable for the words therein.

Word Search

In this and subsequent stages, the Word Search regularly follows the Words and Phrases Checklist. Students should not only match each definition with the correct English word, but also find, in the checklist immediately preceding, the Latin parent word which serves as a matching clue.

Suggestions for Further Work

1 "Imagine you are a business friend of Caecilius and are also interested in other people's houses. Write an account, as though in a letter, of a visit you made to Caecilius at home." When writing this account as an assignment, students may include other characters and even dialogue. If you preface this assignment with a pertinent discussion or with slides or book illustrations of Caecilius' extant house, it will be that much better a learning experience.
2 Younger students may profit from a more creative approach, e.g. writing what they "saw" in Pompeii while flying above through a "time warp" in an "unidentified flying object." These students, though allowed some leeway, should nevertheless describe buildings and layouts that are historically more or less accurate.
3 "Draw up an imaginary 'List of Things to Do Today' which Metella might have kept on a wax tablet." Students can add to this list as they progress through the course and learn more about life in Pompeii in general, and about Metella in particular.
4 Have students construct a spindle for wool out of a dowel rod and a potato, or improvise a loom with a pair of wooden chairs. For instructions, see the Appendix of CSCP, *How the Greeks and Romans Made Cloth*, pp. 59–68.

STAGE 2: IN VĪLLĀ

BRIEF OUTLINE

Reading passages ⎫	
Background material ⎭	social and domestic life
Chief grammatical point	nominative and accusative inflections

NARRATIVE POINTS

Date	Setting	Characters Introduced	Story Line
A.D. 79	Pompeii: Caecilius' house	*amīcus* (merchant), *ancilla*	Dinner party: Grumio eats, drinks, and flirts as host and guest sleep.

GRAMMATICAL POINTS

accusative singular: declensions 1, 2, 3
   e.g. *amīcus canem salūtat.*
superlative adjective
   e.g. *Grumiō est laetissimus.*

SENTENCE PATTERNS

NOM + ACC + V
   e.g. *amīcus Caecilium salūtat.*
NOM + ACC + V *et* V
   e.g. *Grumiō triclīnium intrat et circumspectat.*

Model Sentences

On pp. 20 and 21, a friend visits Caecilius, and the scene is set in the atrium. On pp. 22 and 23, Metella supervises work in the kitchen.

   The accusative is here introduced, not in isolation, but in the context of a very common type of sentence: nominative + accusative + verb. Introduce the situation briefly, "Here, we have a friend, or *amīcus*, visiting Caecilius." Then take each pair of sentences together, in the following manner:

1 Ask students to identify the single character in the left-hand picture and to translate the caption. The latter should present no difficulty, as many similar sentences were met in Stage 1.
2 Next, turn to the right-hand picture and guide the exploration with questions like "Who is approaching Caecilius?" and "What is he doing?"
3 Encourage suggestions for the meaning of the caption *amīcus Caecilium salūtat*. Various translations will be offered, like "greets," "says hello to," and, inevitably, "salutes." Any of these translations, ranging from the colloquial to the formal, will have the effect of establishing the appropriate grammatical relationship ("doer" and "done-to") between *amīcus* and *Caecilium*. At this point, no abstract analysis of the form *Caecilium* is necessary. If students ask "Isn't his name

Caecilius?", confirm that they should continue using the form
"Caecilius" in their English translation.
4 Repeat steps 1–3 with the next pair of sentences.
5 When students have worked through pp. 20 and 21 once, read the
pages again quickly, using two students for each pair of sentences.
Each student reads his or her sentence aloud in Latin and translates
it. Or one student reads both sentences aloud, and the other translates
both.
6 Work through pp. 22 and 23 in the same way.

If students ask about the new inflection, or appear confused or
uncertain, assure them that it *is* a new ending and that they will meet
more examples of it in their reading. For most students, this comment
will suffice until they have read one or both stories in the stage, by which
time they will have the language note to study.

mercātor

The story continues to focus attention on the domestic life of Caecilius,
but makes contact with the larger world outside by bringing a merchant
friend to the house. It tries to give students an impression both of
character and of profession. Caecilius is at work on his accounts in the
tablinum. Grumio, a happy extrovert, is fixing something special for
dinner.
    This and other stories will have greater impact on students if read
aloud with full and careful voice. Good phrasing, dramatic expression,
and well-controlled pace—all these will bring the text to life.
    When leading the students in this first exploration of meaning, teach
them to use the glossary at the end of the story as a reservoir of
information to be tapped when necessary. New words should always be
seen first, not in the glossary, but in context of the story. Then ask
leading questions about the sense of one, two, or three sentences before a
complete translation is given. Follow up hints at character and attitude.
These may be revealed in a sentence like *Caecilius Grumiōnem vituperat*,
with another on its heels like ("in triclīniō") *dominus coquum laudat*. After
the first reading, proceed to integrate, or consolidate, the new bits of
knowledge.

in triclīniō

Continuing the plot from the previous story, "in triclīniō" shows Grumio
and Clemens serving food and wine to Caecilius and his guest. The
slave-girl entertains them by singing, and presently they both fall asleep,
at which point Grumio enters, eats and drinks freely, and flirts with the
slave-girl.

Link this story with the background material at the back of Stage 2. Help students visualize the scene accurately; they need to notice how it resembled and how it differed from a modern dinner party, since they ought to imagine these characters as real people in a social setting and not just as foreign names on a printed page. If students know little about Roman society, they might read the background material at home before you explore the Latin story in class. Refer students, in the textbook, to the diagram and drawing of a triclinium on p. 31; the photograph of the kitchen in the House of the Vettii on p. 29; and the photograph of carbonized walnuts, bread, and grain from Pompeii on p. 28.

Both stories are suitable for dramatic presentation. If time is limited, students may simply walk through their parts, reading their lines from texts in hand. Some students can improvise gestures and expressions that are extremely expressive, and all students will enjoy these.

Language Note

Begin discussion with the class by going back to the model sentences.

TEACHER: Let's take a pair of these sentences and look at the differences between them. Which pair do you choose?

STUDENT: (for example) *Caecilius est in ātriō* and *amīcus Caecilium salūtat*.

TEACHER: (Writes sentences on blackboard; then asks for translations and writes them underneath.) Caecilius appears in both sentences, but there is a difference in the Latin between the ways that he appears. Who can point out the difference?

STUDENT: In one, he is *Caecilius*; in the other, he is *Caecilium*.

TEACHER: Good. Both these Latin words mean "Caecilius," but each has a different form. *Caecilius* is called the nominative case, and *Caecilium*, the accusative case. (Writes case names on the blackboard.) Now look at the sentence containing *Caecilium* and see how it is translated into English. Here are some more sentences. Can you point out more examples of the nominative and accusative case?

Choose sentences that show accusatives including all three endings, *-um*, *-am*, and *-em*. Invite comments. The students may say that the nominative case shows the person who does something; the accusative, the person who has something done to them. Some of them may notice, when they compare a Latin sentence with its English translation, that where Latin uses the accusative, English places the corresponding word at the end of the sentence. If students notice that the accusatives end with *-m*, confirm that this is usually so. After they have had enough time to make their own comments, ask them to study the language note on page 26. Add more examples as needed. Keep from presenting the cases in isolation, but in nominative + accusative + verb word order.

A few students, especially if they studied some Latin previously with teachers who preferred a more abstract approach to the language, may describe the cases in terms of their use, as "subject" or "object." If students apply these terms correctly, confirm their observations. Remember, however, that students may be parroting what they once heard and may have little conscious understanding of what the terms mean. On the whole, students will have a clearer view of the lesson, if you concentrate on the terms "nominative" and "accusative" and their characteristic endings. Get students to study examples of cases in specific sentences (particularly sentences taken from or recalling the stories that they have read). This is more helpful than drilling abstract terms like "subject" and "object."

In a later lesson, you may want to use another reading passage to consolidate the information in the language note. Ask students to pick out nominatives and accusatives by asking questions (on "in triclīniō") "What case is *dominum* in line 6?" or "Which word is nominative in *coquus ancillam spectat*, line 12?" Sometimes follow up by asking for a translation of the sentence under discussion. This translation will remind students of the function of the two cases.

Drills

Exercise 1   Type: completion
              Missing item: noun *or* verb *or* prepositional phrase
              Test of accuracy: sense and word arrangement
              Grammatical point being practiced: structure of simple
                  sentence

Exercise 2   Type: completion
              Missing item: verb
              Test of accuracy: sense
              Grammatical point incidentally practiced: accusative

Sentence 9 of exercise 2 may disclose among students some confusion between *canem* and *cēnam*. The English derivative "canine" may help to disentangle the two words.

Although the choice in some sentences of drills like these two is extremely easy, students will nevertheless benefit from writing out a complete, correct Latin sentence, together with its translation. If the choice were difficult, students—especially if they were working alone at home—would be more likely to write out an incorrect sentence and would not benefit thereby from the exercise.

Exercise 3   Type: translation

After the class has completed exercise 3, you may want to discuss the translations of the sentence *amīcus cibum cōnsūmit*. Write the different translations and their context on the blackboard:

1 Grumio sees the friend. The friend eats the food.
2 Grumio sees the friend. The friend is eating the food.

Ask students to explain the difference, or to say why (2) is here better than (1).

The Background Material

Because students are likely to ask many questions about meals and food, equip yourself ahead of time with detailed information. Consult, for instance, Paoli 92–99 and Balsdon, *Life* 17–55. Roman recipes can be found in Apicius and McLeish. Remember that informal family meals, the *ientāculum*, or breakfast, and *prandium*, or lunch, were eaten while the Romans stood or sat. They reclined on an elbow, on couches, at dinner, particularly if guests were present.

Suggestions for Discussion

1 "During the Roman day, the times of meals and work were somewhat earlier than ours." Ask students to suggest some reasons for this difference. Such suggestions will lead to comments about how artificial light has facilitated changes in social habits. Students descended from or acquainted with families of southern European extraction may note that the daily schedule there is still similar to the Roman one.
2 "How did the Romans tell time? How often did they need to know it?" A sundial is illustrated in filmstrip 11 (slide 10).
3 Refer students to the photographs on pp. 24 and 25 in their textbook (filmstrip 10, 14; slides 16–18), and show photographic plates in other books, or photographs cut from magazine articles, to indicate the kind of decoration that Pompeians often painted on the wall of the triclinium. "What do you think of the idea of paintings of food? What else did Romans paint (cf. photographs on pp. 12, 97, 120; filmstrip 21; slides 37, 43, 45)? What other subjects did they like to have in their murals?"

Suggestions for Further Work

1 "Imagine yourself a tradesman, like a baker, and *cliēns* of Caecilius. If you were a 1st-century Pompeian, how would being a *cliēns* of Caecilius affect your life? Write a dialogue, in English,

of a conversation between you and Caecilius at the morning *salūtātiō*."

2 Junior high or high school students enjoy transforming their classroom into a triclinium. They tape large sheets of poster or shelving paper to the walls. With broad felt-tip pens or with diluted tempera colors, they paint triclinium-style murals of food, dishes, or daily commerce.

3 Many secondary-level schools sponsor an annual "Roman banquet." Murals, like those mentioned in (2), may decorate the walls of the cafeteria, where such affairs are usually staged. Students enjoy dressing up in tunics that can easily be created with white or colored sheets and safety pins (not unknown to the Romans!). The usual foods that students enjoy may be "christened" with Latin names, e.g. "Roman fries" instead of French fries; "peacock-burgers" instead of hamburgers; "Grumio-cola" instead of Coke, and so on. For entertainment, some of the students may present stories dramatized from this or subsequent stories, or their own original playlets or skits. College students have been known to enjoy such goings-on, particularly when they have spring fever! Young people of all ages consider lying on the floor a rare treat, whereas teachers may prefer to sit at a table with visiting parents. Aside from the sense of fellowship derived from a "Roman banquet," students experience the reality of Roman life by recreating it and learn that communal dining and interesting clothes are among the oldest of civilized pleasures.

STAGE 3: PANTAGATHUS, CELER, SYPHĀX

BRIEF OUTLINE

Reading passages Background material	}	Pompeii and its inhabitants
Chief grammatical point		nominative and accusative of 1st, 2nd, and 3rd declensions

NARRATIVE POINTS

Date	*Setting*	*Characters Introduced*	*Story Line*
A.D. 79	Pompeii: Forum	Pantagathus (barber), Celer (painter), Syphax (slave-dealer), Melissa (slave-girl) *poēta*	Celer paints Hercules at Caecilius' house; Pantagathus, angry at poet, cuts customer; Caecilius buys Melissa from Syphax; Metella dislikes her.

attributive adjective
    e.g. *magnus leō est in pictūrā.*
accusative singular in prepositional phrases
    e.g. *pictor ad vīllam venit.*

SENTENCE PATTERN
V + NOM
    e.g. *respondet Pantagathus.*

Model Sentences

Because this stage is designed to help students integrate their previous
knowledge, it contains no model sentences.

in forō

The stories in Stage 3 take the students outside Caecilius' family circle
and introduce them to the town and some of the varied people and
occupations to be found in it. The introductory, descriptive narrative is
set in the forum, the social and business center of the town. (Students
will think of the modern "shopping mall" immediately.) The narrative
introduces the three characters of the main stories in this stage:
Pantagathus the barber, Celer the painter, and Syphax the slave dealer.
In this and the other narratives, you should maintain a rapid pace and
encourage students to practice reading the Latin aloud until they are
quite fluent.

pictor

Celer proceeds to Caecilius' house, where he completes work on a mural
depicting Hercules and a lion. Celer paints murals on commission from
wealthy householders. He is typical of painters in the school of
Campanian artists who, while reproducing Greek mythological
characters and scenes, often from Greek originals, were much more than
hack copyists. Their own sense of style and form, their use of rich color,
made their paintings distinctly theirs and therefore Roman.

    In this story, students will find their repertory of prepositional phrases
expanded from *in ātriō, in tablīnō* etc. to include *ad vīllam* and *ē tabernā.*
Students should learn these phrases as single units, not as words to be
analyzed separately as prepositions with objects terminating in different
inflections. Students will remember them easily as complete phrases.
Additional examples appear in the drills.

Phrases like *magnus leō* and (in the next story) *multus sanguis* constitute a further advance in grammar. The adjective, used in Stages 1 and 2 predicatively in sentences like *coquus est laetus*, is now being used attributively. The attributive use of the adjective does not require comment from you at this point. Students will meet in subsequent stages many more examples of noun + adjective phrases, involving different cases and different declensions. These will be discussed and practiced in the language notes of Stages 14 and 18.

A student playing Celer can easily mime this story, while another student reads the descriptive narrative. The student Celer can draw his or her picture on the blackboard.

tōnsor

Pantagathus, whose name indicates a Greek origin for him, runs a barbershop. Caecilius visits the barbershop, but leaves when Pantagathus gets so angry with a poet who is reciting obscene verses in the shop, that he cuts an elderly customer whom he is shaving.

Throughout history, the barbershop has been a popular, not just a necessary, gathering-place for men. In Pompeii, the barbershop would have been a place where news as well as gossip was exchanged. At the period when this story is imagined as taking place, the Romans were generally smooth-shaved. Normally, rather than shave at home, they visited the barber sometime during the morning. The poet who stops by to recite his obscene verse reminds students that in the Classical world literature was more a public, performing art than it usually is today.

Notice the new word order appearing in some sentences: verb + nominative, e.g. *inquit Caecilius* and *respondet Pantagathus*. This story is a well-known favorite of younger students who love to dramatize it. One or two students have been known to fight for the privilege of playing *tōnsor* with long cardboard razor in hand. You may have to restrain the self-volunteered student-*poēta*, who sometimes can imagine a *scurrīlem versum* only too readily. The student-actors can mime the entire story, except for the greetings, the *versus scurrīlis*, and the outburst, *furcifer*! Students should preferably only imagine the blood that *fluit* over the floor.

Several reading passages in this course are followed by comprehension questions to be answered in English; "tōnsor" is the first such passage. We have designed the questions on the expectation that students will answer them after they have read the entire passage. We might also add that you can and should put together your own comprehension questions for use after any or all stories in the course. The questions provided in the students' textbook, accordingly, will serve as rough models when you are planning ahead your own questions. The final question printed after "tōnsor" is open-ended. There is more than one possible explanation for Caecilius' sudden exit from the barbershop. Students should consider various alternative explanations.

vēnālīcius

Caecilius goes to the harbor where Syphax is selling slaves; he buys Melissa, who is an excellent cook, is learning Latin, and is pretty. Everyone at home is delighted with her except Metella.

Syphax, like Celer and Pantagathus, is an imaginary character. He is presented as a wily Syrian who makes his living buying and selling slaves, and bringing skilled, as well as manual, laborers to the Italian slave-markets. By the time when this story supposedly took place, the number of slaves captured during military conquest had declined. The prices charged by men like Syphax were correspondingly high.

You might ask students, "Why, in line 9, does Syphax call for wine?" Some may see the action of Syphax as a ploy for softening Caecilius up; others, as an excuse to bring Melissa on the scene.

Notice the sentence in the next-to-last paragraph: *Melissa cēnam optimam coquit.* Students often translate this as "Melissa cooks dinner very well." Since Latin frequently employs an adjective in an adverbial manner do not dismiss the above translation as wholly wrong. Rather, ask students to rephrase the translation and slowly guide them to the version, "cooks a very good dinner." You may do this by asking, "What kind of dinner does Melissa cook?" Comprehension questions of this kind, which lead the student very close to the answer, are preferable to long-winded "lectures" on abstract grammar.

The final sentence, *ancilla Metellam nōn dēlectat*, may partially explain why many students see Metella as an unsympathetic character, jealous of Melissa, who is young and attractive. They should also see that Melissa is quite literally the "object" (bought at the market) of Grumio's and Quintus' attention or, possibly, unsolicited affection. Do not allow students to lay facile charges of "male chauvinism." They should attempt to comprehend the familial and psychological problems that slavery, as part of the Roman social system, caused.

The varying origins of Syphax, Pantagathus, and Celer provide the class with an opportunity to discuss the cosmopolitan structure of the Roman empire, reflected typically at Pompeii because of the town's historical growth—Samnite, Greek, and finally Roman occupation—and its trading contacts with the east and west.

Use a story in Stage 3 as the basis for further drill, asking students to pick out nominatives and accusatives, as described above on pp. 30–31.

Language Note

The note in this stage introduces students to the technical term
"declension." Students should come to realize very early that if they can
recognize the case of a word in one particular declension, they will be
able to recognize the same case in other words of that same declension.
For the sake of drill, ask students to identify which word in an English
sentence would, in Latin, be nominative or accusative. They could then
turn to the language note and, with the help of the nominative and
accusative paradigms there printed, tell what the Latin translation
would be, e.g. for "store," in the sentence, "I entered the store"; for
"slave," in "the slave ran"; for "merchant," in "Caecilius sees the
merchant." If the students are very proficient in language-study, ask for
the nominatives and accusatives of words besides those in the paradigms
of the language note.

Drills and Suggestions for Further Practice

Exercise 1   Type: completion
              Missing item: verb
              Test of accuracy: sense

Exercise 2   Type: completion
              Missing item: noun
              Test of accuracy: correct inflection
              Grammatical point being practiced: nominative and
                  accusative singular (introduced in Stage 2)

You might wish, if necessary to clarify students' understanding, to ask
them how they arrived at their choices in exercises like these, especially
those that require selection between inflections of the same word (as in
exercise 2). You should be interested in discovering which students can
explain their choice accurately (*amīcus servum laudat:* "The slave does not
do the praising.") and which students, if they are candid, will admit to
guessing or trusting to a beneficent providence ("I thought that maybe
the second choice would usually be the right one.")

By this time in their progress through the course, students should be
able to comprehend, without translating it, a simple story that they have
read previously. For example, read to them, while they keep their books
closed, the story "Cerberus" in Stage 1, in the way described above,
p. 29.

The Background Material

The street map of Pompeii on p. 43 of the students' textbook provides an
initial view of the physical features and pattern of the town. Using this

map, take the students on a kind of walking tour of Pompeii by inviting them to look at the photographs in their textbook of sites and buildings in Pompeii: pp. 41, 45, 61, 65, and 141 (street scenes); p. 53 (meeting hall of the cloth merchants); p. 56 (basilica); p. 81 (theater); pp. 124 and 130 (amphitheater); and p. 139 (palaestra). Emphasize not only their location, but also their role in the community life of the Pompeians. If the students are in junior high school or in some of the inner-city high schools of the United States where students have little prior knowledge of the world or its history, you might shape your lecture as a tour-talk for new arrivals in a "time machine," or as Grumio's descriptions of Pompeii for the new arrival in Caecilius' household, Melissa. Melissa, as a Greek-born slave, might have appreciated seeing murals copied from Greek originals or attending Latin plays based on Greek originals that she had known in her homeland.

Most students cannot, without having been there, properly imagine the size of Pompeii. Compare its area of 163 acres (66 hectares) with the area of the school's or college's football ground or stadium or other familiar large place.

Explain to students that the Pompeians, like many North American townspeople, expressed their civic pride in public buildings (like the townhalls of New England or the courthouses of the American Middle-West), statues (like those of British kings and queens in Canadian city parks), and inscriptions, not as here "to the Glory of God," but to the civic goddess, "Venus Pompeiana."

You might also want, in order to explain the cosmopolitan sophistication of the town, to outline the earlier period of its growth. Development proper began with the arrival of Greek merchant adventurers in the seventh century B.C., who recognized the advantages of a site that dominated the approaches to the valley of the Sarno river and the fertile Campanian plain just inland. By the sixth century, the Greeks had gained control of the entire gulf of Naples by establishing a series of towns and fortifying hills, including Cumae, Puteoli, Neapolis, down to the peninsula of Surrentum at the southern end of the bay. (Students might be impressed to discover, by looking at a modern map of Italy, that these place names have survived into modern times: Cuma, Pozzuoli, Napoli, and Sorrento.) In the fifth century, the population of Pompeii was further mixed, when the Samnite tribespeople descended from the Apennine mountains, seized the coastal plain, and imposed their own culture on the Greek one.

After Roman armies finally defeated, in 295 B.C., the aggressive Samnite tribes, Pompeii became loosely attached, through an alliance, to Rome. In the Social war in the early part of the first century B.C., Pompeii joined the rebellious Samnite confederacy and tried to throw off its political connection with Rome. But in 89 B.C. Pompeii, after a short siege, fell to Roman soldiers. In 80 B.C., a colony of Roman troops and their families was settled at Pompeii. In accordance with the usual practice when Rome organized a conquered city as a colony, the newcomers confiscated a large proportion of the previous owners' land and property. They also took over the most important magistracies and established Latin as the official language. Inevitably, there were disputes and the new families faced a good deal of entrenched hostility. Gradually, however, the newcomers intermarried with the older families. The old bitterness waned. Pompeii was growing fast. Construction of its amphitheater (the oldest surviving Roman amphitheater) had been started in 80 B.C. on the initiative of the duovirs Quintus Valgus and Marcus Porcius. The same two magistrates also built, at their own expense, the small theater beside the large open-air theater (p. 81 of the students' textbook). A second complex of public baths was built just north of the forum. The town was producing a wealthy and ambitious provincial society.

Under the Emperor Augustus, the city continued to expand. Many wealthy individuals continued to finance various improvements in the town. The forum was paved with limestone slabs; the Temple of Fortuna Augusta was built with extravagant marbles by Marcus Tullius; the open-air theater was enlarged and renovated by the family of Holconii, also with generous amounts of marble; and the magnificent new palaestra, or "sports field," was now developed. It was (and is, see photograph, p. 139) a square field approximately 150 yards (140 meters) along each side, surrounded by colonnades, or porticos. In the center was a large swimming-pool, around which was planted a double line of trees to provide cool and shade for the athletes. An aqueduct, 60 miles (100 kilometers) long, was constructed to bring water from the hills to a group of ten towns ranged around the bay, including Pompeii and Stabiae in the south and Misenum to the north. This aqueduct increased mightily the water supply for Pompeii, which previously had depended on wells and the collection of rainwater in cisterns.

All this activity was suddenly interrupted by the earthquake of A.D. 62, which damaged most public buildings and many private houses. But it is clear from the archaeological evidence that life went on vigorously. Private houses were repaired and became, while being repaired, all the more luxurious. The amphitheater (pp. 124, 130 of students' textbook) and other public buildings were restored, and a new and very large complex of public baths (the Central Baths) was begun. Other buildings, however, like the Temple of Venus and the Temple of Jupiter, were still in a very damaged condition when the final disaster of A.D. 79 brought the life of Pompeii dramatically to its end.

Suggestions for Discussion

1 The similarities and differences in appearance between Pompeii and a modern town. Similarities might include the large sports "palace" (like Houston's astrodome or Montreal's Olympic stadium), compared with the amphitheater; or the prevalence of graffiti on the older buildings of New York City or Philadelphia, compared with those surviving on the walls of Pompeii. (A collection of Pompeian graffiti is included in Marx 17–28.) Differences might include the volume of traffic, the methods of garbage disposal, or the systems of pipes that today are used instead of aqueducts (like those that bring water from the Colorado river to desert-surrounded Los Angeles).

2 Discuss the amenities of life in Pompeii. "Where were the open places for meeting people and walking? What entertainments were available? How did people get about town? On foot, in wagons, in carriages? What did they cook on? Where did they get their water? How was news communicated? How did people know where other people lived? How did strangers locate their destinations within the town?" Considering the comment, on p. 41 of the students' textbook, about the lack of street names or similar identifying marks, some students may be puzzled by the plaques visible in the accompanying photographs. Tell them that these plaques were set up by modern archaeologists (on analogy with modern street signs) to provide a reference system for their grids and maps.

Words and Phrases Checklist

The word *forum*, because it does not have an exact modern counterpart, should be brought over into English directly. The forum was an aggregate of buildings that comprised the civic, legal, mercantile, religious, and social meeting-place of the Romans. The closest equivalents to the Roman forum, in North America, are the civic centers, shopping malls, and renovated historical market-buildings (like those near Boston harbor or in old Omaha).

Conversely, many students will be tempted to translate *vīlla* by the loan word "villa," but remind them that "villa" in North America connotes a country- or resort-house. A house built, like that of Caecilius, in town was, strictly speaking, a *domus urbāna*. In Unit 1, *vīlla* is used as a term of convenience (since the inflections of *domus* are complex) for "(town) house."

Suggestion for Further Work

Duplicate by spirit-copier or mimeograph an outline plan of the town and ask students to label the forum, the theaters, the amphitheater, the large palaestra, the Forum and Stabian baths, the house of Caecilius, the Sea Gate, the main shopping area, and some of the gates. You can keep these completed outline plans and return them at a later time when students can label even more places and structures. The previously written labels will provide a convenient review.

STAGE 4: IN FORŌ

BRIEF OUTLINE

Reading passages ⎫
Background material ⎬ the forum: law and business

Chief grammatical point   1st and 2nd persons singular, present tense

NARRATIVE POINTS

Date	*Setting*	*Characters Introduced*	*Story Line*
A.D. 79	Pompeii: Forum	Hermogenes (Greek merchant)	Hermogenes borrows money from Caecilius, refuses to repay; court scene; Caecilius wins.

GRAMMATICAL POINTS

1st and 2nd persons singular present: all conjugations (including *sum*)
    e.g. *quid tū pingis? ego leōnem pingō.*
adest
·   e.g. *nāvem habeō, sed nāvis nōn adest.*
mē
    e.g. *leō mē spectat.*
questions with no interrogative word
    e.g. *tū ānulum habēs?*

SENTENCE PATTERNS

interrogative word (*quis, quid, cūr, ubi*) + NOM + V
    e.g. *quid tū habēs?*
interrogative word + V + NOM
    e.g. *quis es tū?*

Model Sentences

Characters familiar to the students now begin to speak in the first person. They say who they are, e.g. *ego sum coquus*, and what they are doing, e.g. *ego cēnam coquō.* They also answer the questions *quid?* and *quis?*

We have placed *ego* or *tū* alongside the verb (though this already has a personal ending within it) in order to reduce for students, at this point in their progress, the contrast between Latin and English; however, we phase out these separate pronouns over the succeeding stages.

The grammatical advances in the model sentences present few, if any, difficulties. The words *ego, tū, quis?* and *quid?* are the only new words (until *vēndō*). Because the content of the illustrations provides strong clues to the sense of the sentences, students are unlikely to require much assistance. You might begin by reading the first two model sentences, or Grumio's self-description. Ask the class to tell what Grumio means, perhaps prompting as follows: "Grumio is speaking. What does he say about himself?" Demonstrate *ego cēnam coquō* by setting imaginary cooking utensils on a "stove," pointing at yourself when saying *ego*. Then assign the other sentences to individuals or groups of students, asking them to read the sentences aloud and translate. Lead students to see these first person statements and second person questions as being concerned with the immediate present, not with habitual action, i.e. *quid tū vēndis?* as "What are you selling?" rather than "What do you sell?"

Hermogenēs

Hermogenes, a Greek merchant, borrows money from Caecilius, but refuses to pay it back. Caecilius therefore takes him to court. Help students visualize the actions described in the phrases *cēram habeō, ānulum habeō, ānulus signum habet*, and *signum in cērā imprimō*. Explain, if necessary, the purpose of a signet ring. Hermogenes stamps the raised image of his ring on the wax tablet as an acknowledgement of receipt, and Caecilius keeps the stamped tablet as proof of the transaction. Encourage students to suggest modern analogies, like the rubber-stamped seals used by registered public accountants to certify the transactions they witness. Watch for students who confuse *cēra* with the previous words *cēna* or *canem* (see p. 31).

All the reading passages in this stage introduce the first and second persons of the verb in conversation, where they most naturally occur. Here, to recreate this conversational tone, ask three students to take the parts of the characters. The story "Hermogenēs" requires three people: the narrator, Hermogenes himself, and Caecilius. Each may read his part in Latin, or provide an expressive translation.

in basilicā

When Hermogenes refuses to pay back the money he owes, Caecilius summons him to court and wins the case by producing a wax tablet of the contract with Hermogenes' seal.

Some Suggested Questions

What do you think Caecilius does when he says *ego cēram habeō. tū signum in cērā vides?* (line 24)?

Why does Hermogenes say *ēheu!* (25)? Does he say it aloud?

What is Hermogenes doing when Caecilius says *ecce!* (27)? Why?

What does the judge do just before saying *ecce! ānulus rem probat* (28)?

Five people are needed to take the parts in the story "in basilicā": a narrator for the first sentence, a judge, Caecilius, Hermogenes, and an *amīcus*. Once students have worked out the sense of the story, they should be able to read it aloud all the more dramatically. Junior high school students may quarrel over who receives a part to read out or act. If so, consider presenting the playlet at least twice, once in Latin and once in English. Should students be weak in Latin, they might present their English version before other students present the playlet in Latin. Actors may read their lines from the textbook or from the blackboard where other students have copied them. Students may also copy the text onto an overhead transparency and project it onto the wall that faces the actors, where the text serves as the equivalent of cue cards. We have even observed student "productions" in which an English translation, line by line, was projected onto the wall behind and above the heads of the student-actors. The student monitoring the projector uncovers each line of text as appropriate. The projector-monitor may also periodically flash "scenery" on the wall behind and above the actors (e.g. a drawing of a classical column for "in basilicā") or, in the case of culturally foreign words like *cēra*, a drawing of waxed tablet-boards, flashed temporarily while the student-Caecilius says *ego cēram habeō*. Because such projector-monitors coordinate translation or illustration with the actors' Latin, they must concentrate on the sense—excellent practice for any student, but especially for the student who likes machines more than words (or thinks she or he does!). You might record, on a simple cassette-tape recorder, every reading or performance, and later play parts back. Students enjoy listening to themselves and, without realizing it, receive reinforcement in Latin by hearing the words yet again. Keep the tapes of the best readings or performances. The junior high or high school teacher might consider playing some of these tapes during parents' visitation night. Often parents, particularly those who remember their own Latin classes as torment, are surprised to hear their own children recreating and—goodness!—enjoying Latin. Such parents often read the Units themselves and share in their offspring's pleasure. Such parents also become more effective tutors to their children.

Language Note

Follow up the note with further drill in familiar verbs. Give students examples of other Latin verbs they have studied, say *respondeō*, *respondēs*, and *respondet* accompanied at first by *ego*, *tū* or *servus*, or other by now familiar nouns. Ask them to translate, and if they make errors, discuss the meanings of inflections or write a paradigm on the board. Then repeat the drill of verbs, omitting, this time, the pronouns or nouns. Help the student who is troubled by *currit* after she or he has learned *servus currit*. Point out that "he" may be substituted for "slave" and that the *t*-part of the Latin verb means "he" (as well, depending on context, as "she" and "it").

Drills

Exercise 1   Type: completion
                  Missing item: verb
                  Test of accuracy: sense
                  Grammatical point incidentally practiced: 1st and 2nd
                      persons singular

Exercise 2   Type: translation

The Background Material

Here are some additional notes on certain of the forum buildings; the numerals correspond to those on the forum ground plan printed in the students' textbook, p. 63:

1 Temple of Jupiter. Flanked by two triumphal arches. Seriously damaged in A.D. 62, it had not been rebuilt by A.D. 79 (cf. filmstrip 22; slide 38).
2 Temple of Apollo. The *cella* was built on a high *pōdium*, or platform foundation, in the central courtyard. At the foot of the steps up to the cella, stood the altar, and just to one side was a tall ornamental sundial, donated and dedicated by the duoviri, L. Sepunius and M. Erennius. Here were worshiped Apollo and Diana, each represented by a bronze statue that faced the other across the courtyard.

     On the outside wall of the temple enclosure, in the portico that bounded the west side of the forum, was a recess containing the official standard of weights and measures. This *mēnsa ponderāria* (p. 34 of the students' textbook) "table of weights," had a series of cavities of different sizes cut out of the stone slab. By pouring his purchase in one of these cavities, a person could check that the quantity of grain he had bought really conformed to the official Roman standard.

3 Basilica. In spite of its size, it was roofed; the cross-beams were supported on twenty-eight brick columns surrounding the central nave. The basilica served the double function of a courthouse and financial center. In some ways, it paralleled the modern complex of bank-buildings in the centers of large towns and cities or, on a smaller scale, the stock exchanges in New York City or Toronto. At the western end stood the tribunal where the magistrates sat as judges.

5 Offices. These were occupied by the *duovirī* (the two senior municipal officials, or "town managers"), the *aedīlēs* (or "commissioners" in charge of public works) and *decuriōnēs* (or "council," "town board," or "selectmen"), together with their staff of junior officials and clerks. Here was the municipal headquarters of the town (cf. filmstrip 23; slide 39). Voting in the municipal elections took place in the Comitium, which stood on the southeast corner of the forum, at the end of the strada dell' Abbondanza (shown as the Street of Shops on students' diagram in Stage 3).

7 Meeting hall of the cloth merchants ("Eumachia building"). This formed the headquarters of the association of the *fullōnēs* (wool-finishers, dyers, cleaners of cloth). The cost of the structure had been donated by a wealthy businesswoman named Eumachia. See photographs on p. 53 of students' textbook. The association was probably the largest business group in Pompeii and wielded considerable power in local electoral politics. No fewer than twenty-four electoral notices for the year A.D. 79 specifically mention a fuller.

8 Temple of the emperors. Dedicated in particular to the cult of the most recent emperor; at the time of eruption in A.D. 79, this was Vespasian.

9 Temple of the lares of Pompeii. Possibly built to atone for the earthquake of A.D. 62.

10 Market hall, or Macellum, with little shops both inside and outside its walls. The center of the Macellum was an open courtyard. In it stood a small building with a domed roof and a water-tank. A room at the front of this structure was used for religious ceremonies and one at the back served as a fish market.

The sale of food in the forum, as well as in the specialized market buildings, is attested by pictures that have survived. Venders would set up small stalls there, sometimes no more than a little tray on legs, sometimes like the wooden stalls in modern farmers' markets with canvases over the top. In the open space of the forum and in the porticos, venders would sell fresh fruits and vegetables, poultry, ready-made foods, and drinks. A Pompeian could buy a snack almost anywhere she or he happened to be, either by stopping at one of the many *caupōnae* or simply from the street-venders. The most famous Pompeian taste-treat was undoubtedly *gārum* (fish sauce). Modern persons who like the taste of anchovy sauce might have liked garum.

12 Speakers' platform. See photograph on p. 64 of students' textbook.

Suggestion for Discussion

"What would be the modern equivalent(s) of the forum?" For New England towns, the commons or green might be an appropriate equivalent. In most other areas of North America, several different places would, together, make up an equivalent: the courthouse, the bank, the church, the county fairground, the farmers' market, the grange hall, the union headquarters, etc. Students who have visited Europe or Quebec or whose parents have emigrated from Europe might compare the main squares of Old World towns, where people stroll or lounge at cafés and watch others stroll, especially on Sunday evenings. Students who have visited southern Europe or Latin America might remark that in many, say, Italian or Mexican towns, the open-air *mercato* (It.) or *mercado* (Sp.) in the cathedral square is still held regularly. Textbooks of elementary or intermediate Italian or Spanish almost always contain photographs of such markets.

Words and Phrases Checklist

Explain *cēra* fully to students, namely that it means basically, "wax," and that, part for whole, it is extended to mean "waxed tablet-board." Another Latin word for "wax tablet," also part for the whole, is *tabula*. For an analogy, you might remind students of the times they amused themselves as small children, drawing on cakes of paraffin with the tips of matches. You should also pronounce carefully both "d"s of *reddit*, i.e. *red-dit* (from *reddere*), or students may fall into the bad habit of confusing it with *redit*, a different verb that means "returns" (from *redīre*). Finally, by some kind of reverse but fairly common logic, a few students will translate *vēndit*, not correctly as "sells," but as "buys." Teach students derivatives to fix the meaning in their mind; "vending machine" is a word (and object) they understand easily.

Suggestions for Further Work

1 Many classes of all ages have enjoyed producing, as a group, a tourist's guidebook of Pompeii. Students may draw pictures and maps, or supply these as cutouts from magazines or advertising flyers. Before

compiling the guidebook, students should study the layout of the town, its architecture, and its remains, in books other than their textbook.

2 "Write a short English account of a visit to the forum by Clemens to buy food or by Caecilius to negotiate a business deal at the Eumachia." In this exercise, primarily for younger students, encourage them to develop the character of Clemens or Caecilius as revealed by their bargaining activity. Are they sharp? Or do they let others get the better of them? Ask students to describe the bargaining as a dialogue, interspersing Latin words like *ecce!* or *ēheu!* for flavor.

3 "Draw or paint with watercolors, on several pieces of posterboard, a mural of the forum. Put the colonnades and buildings in the background. Remember that the forum was restricted to pedestrians and so there should be no carts and no mules or horses." Different individuals or groups can contribute different sections to the mural. Such a project may last several weeks. If possible, exhibit this mural, and others similar to it, in the corridors of the high school, where students who have not elected Latin (yet!) may see and appreciate them.

STAGE 5: IN THEĀTRŌ

BRIEF OUTLINE

Reading passages ⎫ Background material ⎭	the theater
Chief grammatical point	nominative plural and 3rd person plural present

NARRATIVE POINTS

Date	Setting	Characters Introduced	Story Line
A.D. 79	Pompeii: Theater	Actius and Sorex (actors),	Holiday play attended by all Caecilius' household except Grumio.
	Lucrio's house	Poppaea (slave girl), Lucrio (her master)	Poppaea has trouble getting Lucrio to go to the play so she can meet her boyfriend Grumio.

3rd person plural present: all conjugations (including *sum*)
    e.g. *puellae sunt in viā.*
nominative plural: declensions 1, 2, 3
    e.g. *senēs dormiunt.*
puer
    e.g. *puer est in viā.*
abest
    e.g. *Lucriō abest!*

SENTENCE PATTERN
NOM *et* NOM + V
    e.g. *fēminae et puellae sunt in turbā.*

Model Sentences

These are grouped into two sections. The first, on pp. 68 and 69, depicts street scenes; the second, on pp. 70 and 71, shows actors and spectators in the theater. The street in the illustrations is a simplified version of the strada dell' Abbondanza (Street of Shops) at a point just east of the intersection with the via di Stabia (Stabiae Street). Nearby is the thermopolium (filmstrip 20; slide 35) and the store with the wooden shutters (cf. p. 141 of students' textbook). The people hurrying along the street are going towards the theater, which is approximately 200 yards (180 meters) away.

The theater, which is the subject of this stage, is the large open-air one with a seating capacity of 5,000 (p. 81 of students' textbook). The picture at the top of p. 70 shows the canvas awning stretched across the auditorium by ropes and suspended from wooden poles set in sockets round the upper edge of the walls. Theater awnings were usually colored; their effect on the sunlight filtering into the theater is vividly described by Lucretius (*De rerum natura* IV.75–83).

These model sentences also highlight, as the new grammatical point, *plurality*. In this stage, plural inflections are restricted to nominative noun-forms and to the 3rd person of the present tense verb-forms. Plural inflections of accusative noun-forms are postponed until Stage 8. The accompanying illustrations provide easy clues to meaning; few students encounter difficulties. After the first reading of the sentences, appoint an individual student to read a singular sentence and, immediately after, appoint a group of students to read together, in chorus, a corresponding plural sentence.

The following words and phrases are new—*puella, puer, in theātrō, spectātor, actor, in scaenā, fēmina, iuvenis* and *plaudit*—but students, in most cases, will easily infer the meanings from the pictures or from obvious English derivatives.

āctōrēs

This passage describes the effect of the arrival in Pompeii of two well-known actors, Actius and Sorex. It is a holiday in Pompeii and, although the businesses and schools are closed, the town is lively. Farmers, shepherds, and sailors swell the normal population, and when a herald announces that Priscus will present a play starring Actius and Sorex, everyone rushes to the theater, including all of Caecilius' household except Grumio.

The amount of new vocabulary is fairly large, so identify plural inflections and lead the students through a careful first reading before proceeding to re-reading activities. When students reach the last sentence, encourage them to speculate on the reason why Grumio stays behind in the house (line 13). Students might also comment on the excitement sparked by the arrival of the actors (who were probably *pantomīmī*), and they might compare the enthusiasm that accompanies the concerts of pop-idols today.

Poppaea

Poppaea, a slave girl, is waiting for her boyfriend; she is startled to find that her aged master, Lucrio, is still at home. She wakes the old man up, and finally gets him to understand that a play is being presented that day. As Lucrio hurries off to join the crowd, the boyfriend enters. It is none other than Grumio!

Students, after the first reading, may easily dramatize this story. Select three students to play, respectively, Poppaea, Lucrio, and *amīcus* (alias Grumio); divide the remainder of the class into choruses of *agricolae* and *puerī*. During the read-throughs preceding the dramatic presentation, encourage the actors to feel excitement, to simulate the tension of people hurrying to the theater, Poppaea's impatience, the irritation of Lucrio whose sleep has been disturbed, and his drowsy unawareness of what is happening. Do this by questioning the students and leading them to the parts of the text that best express these states. You can help students improve their understanding with such a read-through, even if they do not go on to memorize parts and present the story as a play.

First Language Note (Plural Forms)

Here, the change from singular to plural is seen in the context of a whole sentence. After the class has met several examples of singular sentences and plural sentences, initiate discussion and/or ask students to study the first two paragraphs of the language note. Invite comments on the ending of the final word of each sentence, and lead the students to notice for themselves the regular *-t/-nt* inflection of the verbs. (Do not, at this time, compound the difficulty of the grammar by attempting explanations of the variation between conjugations.) Continue drilling with additional practice examples, either verb-forms from the checklists in Stages 1–4 or those in paragraph 3 of this language note. Be sure to present verb examples in the context of complete sentences, e.g. not *habet*, but *fēmina canem habet*, and so forth. Later, drill students in verbs alone, e.g. *currit, ambulant, sedent* etc. Remind students, if necessary, that "they" is required when translating plural verb-forms that do not have separate subjects stated.

Drills

Exercise 1   Type: completion
　　　　　　　Missing item: verb
　　　　　　　Test of accuracy: correct inflection
　　　　　　　Grammatical point being practiced: 3rd person plurals, introduced in current stage
　　　　　　　Grammatical point incidentally practiced: nominative plural

In Exercise 1, all nominative nouns are plural. Exercise 2 contains a mixture of nominative singular and plural nouns, and some students may require help. If you think it advisable, precede the exercise with study of the second language note.

Exercise 2   Type: completion
　　　　　　　Missing item: verb
　　　　　　　Test of accuracy: correct inflection
　　　　　　　Grammatical point being practiced: 3rd person singular and plural introduced in current stage
　　　　　　　Grammatical point incidentally practiced: nominative singular and plural

Exercise 3   Type: translation

Second Language Note (Nominative Plural)

This note is designed to confirm that plurality is a feature, not only of the verb, but also of the noun, or to put it in terms more suitable for students a nominative is either nominative singular (e.g. *amīcus*) or nominative plural (*amīcī*). Write on the blackboard additional singular and plural sentences of the nominative + verb pattern. Ask students to translate these sentences and then to point out nominative singulars and nominative plurals, using verb-endings as clues or confirmations. If the class seems secure and confident in their knowledge, comment more fully on singular and plural inflections of the various declensions and, perhaps, drill students in translating nominative singular and plural noun-forms in isolation. If students seem uncertain, however, postpone such discussion and drill until the students have seen more examples of the different inflections in their reading.

The Background Material

On the theater and actors, Balsdon, *Life* (especially 252–61, 270–88) is invaluable. Filmstrip 26, 27 (slides 46–49) are concerned with the theater and theatrical activity.

Theaters were an established part of life in the Roman Republic, and on their stages the comedies of Plautus and Terence and some of the old Roman tragedies were regularly performed. During the Empire, the popularity of theatrical presentations increased still more and every town of any importance had its theater. But the quality of the entertainment changed as public taste declined. The writing of serious drama for the stage seems to have ended in Republican times, and although Plautine comedies were occasionally revived, the most popular performances were of pantomime, mime, and farce.

But although the crowds who turned out in Pompeii to welcome actors like Actius and Sorex did not expect or desire entertainment of great dramatic quality, students should remember that, in Pompeii, the small covered theater, or *ōdēum*, was built during the Augustan period for more serious performances of music and poetic recitations. This theater, like a modern chamber-music concert, would attract support from the more educated elements of Pompeian society.

The photograph on page 79 is of a marble relief in the Naples Museum, illustrating a scene from Greek New Comedy. On it appear some of the characters who later appeared in the comedies of Plautus and Terence. On the right: a drunken young man, supported by a slave and waving the ribbon he had worn at a party. The girl playing the pipes has obviously been to the party as well. On the left: the angry father and his elderly friend who seems to be trying to calm him down.

Words and Phrases Checklist

Inform students that *agit* changes its English meaning, depending on what kind of object it has, as here in *fābulam agit*, or "acts (in) a play" (for other examples, see under *agit* on p. 214 of the students' textbook). The word *agit* means, basically, "drives," and it is related to *agitat* (checklist, Stage 8), or "chases, hunts."

Suggestions for Further Work

1 Read in translation a scene from the *Mostellaria* (The Haunted House), e.g. lines 363–406 (the announcement of Theopropides' return).

2 Allow students to read through scenes from any of the extant Roman comedies in translation, either by Plautus or Terence. Assign parts and, if there is time, let students walk through their parts at the front of the room.

   Junior high school students enjoy reading or acting out the simple, but polished reworkings of Roman comedies (and Greek tragedies) in Cullum. These ready-made English versions are ideal vehicles for class discussion later about the "generation gap," distinctions among social classes and the dangers of unrestricted merrymaking.

3 In college or university, students may present written or oral reports on the history of the Greek and Roman theater, both physical and literary. All students at the collegiate institute level or higher should research the differences between the Roman *mīmus* and *pantomīmus*. The *pantomīmus* Paris appears in stories later in the course.

4 Show a videotape of the Hollywood feature film. *A Funny Thing Happened on the Way to the Forum* 1966: Richard Lester, a pastiche of plots from the *Pseudolus, Casina, Miles gloriosus* and other plays by Plautus.

STAGE 6: FĒLĪX

BRIEF OUTLINE

Reading passages ⎱ Background material ⎰	slaves and freedmen
Chief grammatical point	3rd person singular and plural, imperfect and perfect

NARRATIVE POINTS

Date	*Setting*	*Characters Introduced*	*Story Line*
A.D. 79	Pompeii: Forum	Freedman Felix	Quintus rescues Clemens and Grumio from dog. Clemens witnesses fight between farmer and Greek merchant, meets Felix in
	Tavern Caecilius' house		tavern, invites him home. Story is told of how Felix earned his freedom by saving the infant Quintus from a kidnapper.

GRAMMATICAL POINTS

3rd person singular and plural, imperfect and perfect (*v*-stems)

    e.g. *servī per viam ambulābant, canis subitō lātrāvit.*

erat, erant

    e.g. *Clēmēns erat fortis. servī erant laetī.*

SENTENCE PATTERNS

NOM + Q (subord. adv. clause: *postquam, quod, ubi* (= where)) + ACC + v

    e.g. *coquus, quod erat laetus, cēnam optimam parāvit.*

NOM + ACC *et* ACC + v

    e.g. *Clēmēns Caecilium et Metellam quaesīvit.*

Model Sentences

In these sentences, a fierce dog attacks Grumio and Clemens in the street. Quintus rescues them.

    Although the verbs are either imperfect or perfect tense, no adverbs (e.g. *heri*) appear to help fix the time in the past. You may have to warn students outright about the change, from previous stages, in the tense. Our experience indicates, however, that students are likely to translate sentences about a past Pompeii in the past tense. In subsequent stages, therefore, when the present tense is mixed with the past tenses, you may have to remind students, while they are translating, not to change inadvertently present-tense verbs into past-tense forms.

The two past tenses, imperfect and perfect, are presented in a context that contrasts the situational aspect of the imperfect with the simpler, momentary aspect of the perfect. "The slaves were walking" when "the dog barked." An interruption of a situation by an action or an event is natural in both Latin and English, and is characteristic of these two tenses. Until the aspectual differences in these two past tenses are clear in their minds, students should at first translate imperfect tenses with the English formula, "was -ing" or "were -ing." Later, students should experiment with other variations. Delay class discussion about the difference between continuous state and momentary event in past tenses until students have seen many examples of each. In the meantime, students need only understand the difference between the two tenses in terms of their English translation.

In this stage, the perfect-tense verbs have only the form with -*v*-. Other formations of the perfect will appear in subsequent stages.

The following words are new: *timēbat, superāvit,* and *pulsāvit* (new meaning).

pugna

Clemens goes to the forum, where he observes a fight between a farmer and a Greek merchant. This episode contains simple statements of situation and rapid action in past time. You should slant your comprehension questions to bring out in the students' answers the difference between the imperfect and perfect, thus:

Where was Clemens walking?
What did the farmer do to the Greek?
What were the Pompeians doing?

Help students with the subordinating conjunctions *quod, postquam,* and (in the third story) *ubi* (= where). Because these words are rather colorless, students may fail, initially, to grasp them, particularly *postquam* which is easily confused with *post*. Experience, for some students, is the only cure.

Some Suggested Questions

Why did Clemens hurry when he heard the noise?
Why did the Pompeians back the farmer?
Which Latin word tells you that the fight went on for a long time?
  (Answer: *tandem*)

Fēlīx

Clemens enters a tavern, where he meets Felix, a freedman whom he knows. He invites Felix home, where he is greeted warmly by Caecilius and his family. Felix is moved by the appearance of Quintus. Grumio joyfully cooks an excellent meal.

See p. 10 above for examples of possible questions you may ask when leading a class through the first paragraph of this story. Notice, in the second paragraph, the moment of obvious emotion, when Felix first meets Quintus: *paene lacrimābat; sed rīdēbat* (line 9). Let the class comment and, if they want, speculate briefly on the reasons for the feelings of Felix. The full explanation will emerge, however, in the next story. When students have reached that point, they should be referred back to this point and reminded that the explanation was foreshadowed by this highly affectionate meeting. Finally, ask students why Grumio, in the last line, was so happy. (Comprehension questions like these can sharpen the students' perception of character and situation.) Grumio's pleasure at Felix's arrival suggests Felix's previous position as an established member of Caecilius' household and, therefore, close associate (and evidently friend) of Grumio.

Fēlīx et fūr

After dinner Quintus remarks that Felix was a former slave of Caecilius and wants to know why his father set him free. Caecilius tells the story, with help from Felix himself: Once Felix was alone in the house with an infant. He was so engrossed in his work that he failed to notice a thief entering the house. After looking around, the thief tried to leave quietly with the infant. Alerted by the infant's cries, Felix caught the thief and beat him severely, thereby saving the infant, who was Quintus.

After preliminary exploration and the first reading, students should dramatize this story. Two students, seated, may read the parts of Caecilius and Felix. While Caecilius relates the story of the near-kidnapping, two other students may mime the actions of Felix and the thief (any convenient object may simulate the baby). Should the mimers be uncertain what to do during the fight with the newspaper-roll baby (or whatever baby may be) they might be advised simply to lay "him" down on the floor, out of harm's way. Particularly rambunctious mimers, however, sometimes have other ideas. Be forewarned!

Language Note

When students are studying this and other language notes, they should arrive at a rule or observation by themselves rather than receive it ready-made from you. For example, when the class is considering the imperfect, you should not point out, but rather bring out from the students the rule-observation that the endings -*bat* and -*bant* correspond to the English forms "was -ing" and "were -ing." You might ask able or older students, "What do you notice about the two past tenses?"; less able or quite young students, "Can you work out a rule for translating?" Students may remember a rule handed down to them by you; they are far more likely to remember and apply a rule that they themselves or their class peers have reached. Remembering a rule is not necessarily the same as applying it.

Students should follow study of the language note with oral translation of additional practice examples. Place 3rd person imperfect and perfect verb-forms in complete sentences. Focus on one contrast at a time: thus, examples of imperfect singulars should be contrasted with imperfect plurals (e.g. *petēbat* and *petēbant*). Then imperfect singulars should be contrasted with perfect singulars that contain -*v*- (e.g. *petēbat* and *petīvit*); then imperfect plurals with perfect plurals that contain -*v*- (e.g. *petēbant* and *petīvērunt*). Finally, all these types should be mixed. Remember always to place these verbs in a context (e.g. *canis puellam petēbat*). Later, probably towards the end of Stage 6 or the beginning of Stage 7, repeat this drill. If the students are sure of the differences, present the verb-forms by themselves, saying that the subject be specified, for purposes of drill, as "he" or "they", later as "she" or "they."

Drills and Suggestions for Further Practice

Exercise 1   Type: comprehension

The drill-story "avārus" is not easier than the other stories in Stage 6; you may therefore have to help the class read through it. If so, students should return to this drill-story again later and translate it by themselves.

Exercise 2   Type: completion
                  Missing item: noun
                  Test of accuracy: singular and plural inflections
                  Grammatical point being practiced: nominative singular
                     and plural, introduced in Stage 5

You might follow up these drills with further work, asking students for oral translations of the singular and plural inflections of nominative-case nouns. (At this stage of their progress, students may prefer to see examples written on the blackboard or projected from an overhead transparency.) Choose familiar nouns, particularly those appearing in the earlier checklists (consult Cumulated List of Checklist Words on pp. 114–16 below). Dwell on examples of the 3rd declension, since these are somewhat more difficult than those of the 1st and 2nd declension (e.g. *canis* and *canēs*, *clāmor* and *clāmōrēs*, *leō* and *leōnēs*, etc.).

If time allows, you might also write on the blackboard mixed pairs of nouns and verbs, with nouns in one, verbs in the other column:

puella	*ambulant*
iuvenēs	*coquit*
servus	*clāmat*

Students, by observing sense and inflections, should select the most suitable pairs. Repeat this exercise later with verbs in the imperfect and perfect tenses.

The Background Material

For further information, see Balsdon, *Life* 106–15, D'Arms 72–96, 121–48, and Paoli 120–27. On legal and economic aspects, there is much helpful detail in Finley 62–94 and Hopkins. Slaves, freedmen and poor free men would have worked together in many of the shops and business houses of Pompeii. Tanzer provides much valuable detail about these occupations.

The purpose of the discussion in the students' textbook, at the end of Stage 6, is to introduce with enough detail two features of Roman society, slavery and freedmen, that have no exact counterpart in present-day western society and that can easily be misunderstood. The condition and role of slaves in Roman society was complex; it differed in different places and times; it varied between individual masters; it covered a range of experience from indulgent affection, respect, and mutual confidence, to distrust, resentment, and extreme brutality. As an institution, slavery needs to be explained in terms of actual Roman practice, rather than by analogies with slavery in other (often more modern) societies. Students generally find Clemens and Grumio sympathetic figures and are bothered by the harsher realities of slave life, but, while it is unnecessary to dwell on brutality, you should guide the discussion toward a balanced realism. Slavery as a topic will appear again, in greater detail, in later Units.

For documents relating to two slave sales, see Lewis and Reinhold II, 218–20. Cowell 97 and Dilke, *Ancient Romans* 55 give examples of the cost of slaves. The normal cost range in the first century went from about 800 to about 8,000 sesterces, but the price of especially gifted or attractive slaves could be far higher; the highest recorded price is the 700,000 sesterces paid for the grammarian Lutatius Daphnis, who was immediately set free.

Students often ask what the modern equivalents are for such sums, but the difference between ancient and modern conditions makes direct comparisons meaningless. It may be better to compare other sums from Classical times; for example, in the late first century A.D., a legionary's annual pay was 1,200 sesterces (300 denarii), the maximum fee permitted for a lawyer was 10,000 sesterces and the property qualification for membership of the senate was 1,000,000 sesterces. Compare also the sums quoted from Caecilius' tablets on p. 24 above.

Suggestions for Discussion

1 "What kind of relationship does there seem to be between Caecilius and his slaves in the stories you have read so far? What sort of jobs did the slaves in his household perform? What other work was done by slaves in Pompeii?"
2 "What kind of difficulties would face a slave who was brought into Roman society from a distant country as a young adult?"
3 "What aspects of Grumio's life as a slave would you have disliked? What compensations would you have found in the hardships of Grumio's life?"

Words and Phrases Checklist

You should realize that *lībertus*, without considerable prior discussion, is likely to be quite meaningless to students. There is simply no counterpart in our society. As a result, students can cling to a translation of desperation, like "libertine." If they do, ask them to look up in a dictionary, like *The American Heritage Dictionary*, the etymology of *libertine* (Latin *lībertīnus* from *lībertus*) and discuss the possible reasons for this English adjective coming to describe someone "who acts without moral restraint."

Suggestions for Further Work

1 "Write an imaginary letter from Felix, shortly after gaining his freedom, (a) to Caecilius, and (b) to a fellow freedman." Discuss the different points of view he might express in these two letters.
2 College or university students, especially if their immediate families have emigrated to North America, might want to compare the dual loyalties of freedmen to their former owners and their new life, with the dual loyalties of immigrants to their native homelands and cultures and to the life of the New World. Such new citizens, once they are established in North America, periodically visit their homelands, as Felix visited Caecilius' household.

STAGE 7: CĒNA

BRIEF OUTLINE

Reading passages	social and domestic life (continued from Stage 2)
	Roman supernatural and religious beliefs
Background material	Roman supernatural and religious beliefs
Chief grammatical points	sentences with subject omitted
	further forms of the perfect tense

NARRATIVE POINTS

Date	Setting	Characters Introduced	Story Line
A.D. 79	Pompeii: Caecilius' house	Decens (guest), ghost of dead gladiator Pugnax	Felix, at Caecilius' banquet, tells story of werewolf. Decens fails to arrive, is killed by ghost of Pugnax.
	Woods on Mt. Vesuvius	Gaius	Quintus and Gaius go boar-hunting; Quintus kills boar.
	Pompeii: Caecilius' house		Metella consoles Melissa, who has been scolded by Grumio and Clemens.

GRAMMATICAL POINTS

perfect tense (other than *v*-stems)

    e.g. *amīcī optimum vīnum bibērunt. tandem surrēxērunt.*

tē

    e.g. *ego tē laudō, quod mē dīligenter cūrās.*

hic

    e.g. *Quīntus, postquam ad hanc vīllam vēnit, ātrium intrāvit.*

ille

    e.g. *ille centuriō erat versipellis!*

oblique cases of *is*

    e.g. *gladiātor tamen dominum ferōciter petīvit et eum ad amphitheātrum trāxit.*

accusative of *rēs*

    e.g. *tum amīcus rem intellēxit.*

questions with *num*

    e.g. *num tū timēs?*

SENTENCE PATTERN

ACC + V (suppression of subject)

    e.g. *vīllam intrāvit.*

Model Sentences

Caecilius and a friend have dinner together.

    The most important new feature of these model sentences is the absence, in several sentences, of a subject specified separately from the personal ending within the verb-form. In each sample, the subject to be understood is the same as the subject expressed in the sentence immediately preceding. You should, therefore, identify the subject, when it is not specified, by referring students back to the subject specified in the previous sentence (e.g. the subject of *nārrāvit* in *tum fābulam nārrāvit* is the *amīcus*, who in the previous sentence *pōculum hausit*). Use sequential comprehension questions in order to encourage students to remember, i.e. carry over the subject from one sentence to the next: "What was Caecilius doing? What did he do next?"

    After this kind of dialogue, you should assign the model sentences for translation in class, but assign pairs of sentences so that students become aware that every alternate sentence implies the subject of the previous one. If the students are quite young, ask them to raise their hands each time they hear a student, while reciting, specify a subject in noun form. "Raise your hand whenever you hear someone name the subject exactly (rather than refer back to it)." This latter exercise is particularly effective when students are reading the model sentences in Latin;

simultaneously, they learn to distinguish nouns from other parts of speech; nominative inflections from accusatives.

With younger students, do not discuss the additional ways of forming the perfect tense here illustrated (with -*s*-, -*x*-), unless, of course, students comment on or ask about them. If possible, postpone such discussion until after students have read "post cēnam," when the language note provides a table of various perfect-formations and contrasts them with equivalent imperfect forms. College and university students are usually capable of turning immediately from the model sentences to the second language note. Encourage them, however, to summarize by themselves through discussion the rules implied by the examples. Ask college and university students searching questions, like "Were the perfects *dīxērunt* and *discessērunt* formed in the same way?" (Answer: Yes; they both add the -*s*-, though in *dīxērunt* this -*s*- is hidden in the *x*—it is heard, but not seen.) "Were the perfects *dormīvērunt* and *appāruērunt* formed in the same way?" (Answer: Yes; insofar as -*v*- is related to -*u*- as semivowel (*w* in English *wet*) to vowel (*u* in English *put*), they both add the -*u*-.) See Allen 40–41.

The pictures accompanying the model sentences incorporate several cultural details, like the foods eaten at different courses of the meal, the reclining position of the diners and the lantern that the departing guest holds to light his own way home. Vary the pace of your class by interspersing questions about these items with questions about more abstract matters like understood sentence-subjects and ways of forming the perfect.

Help students with the following new words: *pōculum, īnspexit, hausit, surrēxērunt, valē.* Use the illustrations and plot-line, as much as possible, to help students understand their meaning.

fābula mīrābilis

This story introduces a group of narratives about werewolves, ghosts, and other such spooks. Felix attends a banquet at Caecilius' house. After the meal, Caecilius sends Clemens to look for Decens, a guest who did not show up as expected. Felix tells an eerie tale of a werewolf.

Set the mood of mystery right at first, pointing out that the invited guest Decens is missing.

The Romans were partial to stories of this kind, and liked to tell them after dinner—the ancient equivalents, one supposes, of modern television fantasies about the supernatural. Belief in ghosts, however, as revenants or spirits of dead persons, was probably more widespread then than now. Belief in ghosts was closely connected with popular views about the afterlife and the shadowy survival of the dead.

The original of "fābula mīrābilis" is found in Petronius, *Satyricon* 62, and you may wish to read it in translation to the class because of its details. The original version, a tale told by a dinner-guest, Niceros, illustrates the popular belief that a werewolf, if wounded, retains the wound even after he reoccupies his human form.

Needless to say, you should read or encourage the students to read "fābula mīrābilis" and subsequent stories with appropriately suspenseful tone. We once observed a class of junior high school students whose teacher turned out the lights and read the Latin by flashlight. The word *ululāvit* (line 13), particularly, if extended and wailed as "OOH-LOO-LAAAAAA-vit", evokes a shudder or two if the room is fairly dark.

First Language Note (Sentences with Subject Omitted)

Until students have seen several examples of this type of sentence, you would be well advised, when drilling orally, to usher in each sentence of the accusative + verb pattern with a related sentence in which the subject is specified. See, for example, the paired sentences in the section of model sentences or in paragraph 3 of this language note. Should the students, especially younger students, have difficulty with e.g. *Grumiōnem salūtāvērunt*, do not rush into an abstract analysis of the sentence as "accusative, verb, and implied nominative." Rather, treat the sentence as a single unit of meaning and compare it with *lībertī Grumiōnem salūtāvērunt*.

Decēns

The dinner-guests applaud Felix's tale, but a sudden noise draws them to the atrium, where Clemens and the slaves of Decens tell a horrible story. Decens, en route to the dinner, was attacked and killed by a gladiator. Caecilius further alarms the guests by telling them that the gladiator, Pugnax, is dead and that Decens has been killed by the ghost of Pugnax.

High school students, after their first reading of this story, can easily dramatize it. A narrator and four actors are needed; the entire class may impersonate the banqueters who react with *ēheu* at the news of Decens' death. An off-stage voice (in the classroom: a young student under your desk) may echo, in suitable unearthly tones, the words of Decens quoted by his slave, *tū es īnsānus. ego nōn sum leō. sum homō.*

Should certain students be rationalists to the point of rejecting the supernatural even in fiction, they might be invited to suggest alternative explanations for events in the story. "Could Decens' slaves have been the real murderers? Could Decens have suffered a heart attack? What is your proof? Who wrote this story? Is it traditional, or did a member of the

Cambridge School Classics Project make it up?" You might draw parallels between the anonymity of this story's origin and that of myth, a kind of narrative that is usually incapable of proof or disproof.

After this inquiry into epistemology, you should return to grammar, perhaps using the story (like the others in this stage) as the basis for a substitution exercise like that described on p. 56. For example:

"What does *audīvērunt* (line 2) mean? What would *audīvit* have meant?"

"What does *intrāvit* (line 25) mean? What would *intrābat* have meant?"

With most students, you should change only one variable at a time, i.e. you might change the number of the verb, while keeping the tense unchanged; or change the tense, while keeping the number unchanged.

post cēnam

The terrified guests depart, tip-toeing through the dark night. A cat's howl sends them screaming through the town, to the consternation of many Pompeians. Caecilius, however, sleeps soundly.

While maintaining a mood of mystery, you should redouble in students their expectation of the unexpected, thus setting them up for the deliberate comedown of the howling cat.

Most students will comprehend this short story without translating it, particularly if a dramatically able student reads it aloud with good phrasing and expression and you ask comprehension questions. For example, you might ask, "Why were the friends advancing quietly through the town? What all of a sudden happened? Were the friends frightened? What were they making? What effect did this have on many Pompeians? Did Caecilius hear the uproar? Why not?"

After you have established the surface meaning, you might ask more detailed questions. For example, after *subitō fēlēs ululāvit*, you might ask, "Why did the caterwauling frighten Caecilius' friends while they were going home from the dinner?" (Answer: There were no stars or moon, and their lamps were small. Every noise became a mystery.)

In our experience, young students (and often older ones too) ask what sounds animals make in Latin. If this happens, other animals and their sounds (in the perfect tense) might be orally substituted for *fēlēs ululāvit*, like *ovis* (sheep) *bālāvit, porcus* (pig) *grunnīvit, canis* (dog) *lātrāvit*, or for comic relief *rāna* (frog) *coaxāvit*. Finally, you might ask, "Why, since this howl (or grunt or bark) was sudden and unexpected, is the perfect tense more suited to it than is the imperfect?"

Second Language Note (Further Forms of the Perfect, Contrasted with the Imperfect)

After students have studied this note, you might drill them further with oral examples of perfect and imperfect verbs chosen from the checklists in this or previous stages (consult Cumulated List on pp. 114–16 below). We suggest, particularly, *cōnspexit* (Stage 7), *coxit* (4), *habuit* (4), *intellēxit* (7), *plausit* (5), *prōcessit* (7), *scrīpsit* (6), *surrēxit* (3) and *terruit* (7). All these perfects are formed like the perfects listed in this language note. You should alternate, first regularly, then irregularly, these perfects with equivalent imperfects (e.g. *cōnspexit/cōnspiciēbat, coxit/coquēbat, surrēxērunt/surgēbant* and *terruērunt/terrēbant*). At first, ask students to translate (e.g. "caught sight of/kept catching sight of"), supplying the pronoun "she" or "he" or "they"; then ask them to identify the tense (perfect/imperfect). Do not attempt at this point, unless the students are adults, to force them into distinguishing among the conjugations or within the third conjugation (e.g. *coquēbat* vs. *cōnspiciēbat*). This kind of formal analysis becomes easier for most students after they have seen, read and translated many examples of the various conjugations.

Drills

Exercise 1   Type: completion
Missing item: accusative + verb *or* prepositional phrase + verb
Test of accuracy: sense and correct number-inflection
Grammatical point being practiced: 3rd person singular and plural of perfect tense, introduced in Stage 6

Exercise 2   Type: completion
Missing item: noun
Test of accuracy: correct inflection (case or number)
Grammatical point being practiced: nominative and accusative singular, introduced in Stage 2; nominative singular and plural, introduced in Stage 5

vēnātiō

Quintus is taken on a boar hunt by his friend Gaius, and distinguishes himself. Their game is a ferocious boar on the slopes of Mount Vesuvius. When the boar breaks cover and charges, the slaves flee. Quintus stands firm and slays the fierce animal with his spear.

Because hunting was one of the regular sports of nobles and other wealthy people, their sons would have been trained to ride horses and handle hunting-weapons as soon as they were old enough. See Balsdon, *Life* 219–20, for reference to hunting, and 161–63 for a discussion of the sporting and para-military activities of the youth group *"Iuventūs"* organized by Augustus. Paoli 243–48 describes the techniques of hunting and fishing. Refer students to the photograph of a boar hunt on p. 108 of their textbook. It depicts part of a relief on the side of a Roman sarcophagus, now used as a holy water font in the Cathedral of Cosenza, Italy. Perhaps it depicts the mythical Meleager, Atalanta, and other heroes hunting the Calydonian Boar.

Students will understand the subtle pressure exerted by Gaius on Quintus when he says, *"servī meī sunt ignāvī; aprum timent. num tū timēs?"* Ask them, for example, "Why would Quintus now find it hard to refuse Gaius' invitation to the hunt?" Because some students are accustomed, naturally, to think of Vesuvius as a rather bare volcano, remind them that this hunting episode is imagined as occurring *before* the eruption, when the mountain was heavily forested. Also draw students' attention to Quintus' skill at spear-throwing—a skill that will serve him well when he saves King Cogidubnus from a bear in Stage 16.

The *ex* form of *ē* here appears for the second time (it first appeared in "fābula mīrābilis"), but students have already met *ē* several times. Write *ex ōre* (line 17), *ex urbe* ("fābula mīrābilis," line 8), and *ē vīllā* ("fābula mīrābilis," lines 4 and 6). Ask students to study the examples and suggest a formula for using *ex* or *ē*. You should be aware, though you may prefer not to mention the matter now, that sometimes this formula (*ē* before consonants; *ex* before vowels) was ignored by ancient writers. If necessary mention parallel English constructions, like "*a* village" but "*an* urban development."

Metella et Melissa

Metella finds Melissa crying in the garden. The other slaves, Grumio and Clemens, are dissatisfied with her work in the kitchen and the study. Metella comforts her, however, and praises her for her skill as a hairdresser.

The sharp contrast between the censorious mood of Grumio and of Clemens and the complimentary tone of Metella makes this story an easy playlet for young students to walk through at the front of the room (holding their books) or to memorize for production. Students, should they want to extemporize costumes, might be allowed to drape sheets or curtains about themselves as they choose. At this stage, learning Latin is more important than authentic costumes, although many teachers have been surprised how attractively even young students can drape their sheets. Students always comment on the comparative ease of clothes-making in antiquity.

Third Language Note (Further Forms of the Perfect, Contrasted with the Present)

Perfect forms in this language note are formed by change in root (e.g. *fac-* to *fēc-* or *cap-* to *cēp-*). Because this formation sometimes eludes beginners, the note contrasts the perfect forms, not with imperfects, but with the somewhat similar present forms. You should read out the contrasted forms very carefully, distinguishing, say, between the short "a" in *facit* and the long "ē" in *fēcit*. After the students have read this note, drill them orally (books closed) with these examples and parallel ones from *agit* (Stage 4). If students more frequently translate correctly *agunt/ēgērunt* than they do *agit/ēgit*, ask them why. At least one student will notice that there is one syllable more in the perfect-plural ending *-ērunt* than there is in the present *-nt*, whereas in the third person singular the ending is *-t* in both tenses.

The Background Material

For Roman superstitions see Paoli 279–91, and for beliefs about life after death, funeral rites, and wills see Paoli 128–32 and Balsdon, *Life* 26–29. Refer students to p. 112 of their textbook for a photograph of tombs.

Remind students that the span of life-expectancy in Roman times was shorter than it is today. The Romans were regularly reminded of the brevity of life, and they quite naturally gave considerable attention to the customs, memorials, and monuments by which they hoped posterity would remember them.

Death as a topic may seem rather depressing to junior high or high school students and should not be carried too far, since it is either remote from their experience, or, sometimes, too painfully close. College and university students, however, can generally discuss death philosophically, particularly the irony of material gear which the ancients sometimes supplied for the spirits of the dead.

Suggestions for Discussion

1 "Why do you think that archaeologists often learn much about the daily life of the Romans by excavating the tombs of their dead?"
2 "What kinds of notices and memorials do we use today for somebody who has died? How do they resemble the memorials of the Romans?"
3 "Do you, your family, or friends believe or half-believe in superstitions? What are they?" Consider students' superstitions especially, like wearing a baseball cap during examinations for good luck.

Suggestion for Further Work

Ask a student to read the werewolf story in Petronius, *Satyricon* 62, and report on it to the class. The translation by William Arrowsmith (New American Library) is particularly lively and well annotated. Given the racy and sometimes explicit themes of the entire work, you should consider the students' (or parents') attitudes to sexuality or obscenity before assigning the entire work in translation for reading and/or report. At the college and university level, however, moral strictures or objections are less likely. This being the case, older students can learn much about the strata of Roman society or the particulars of formal dining and exotic food from this celebrated work of Roman prose fiction.

STAGE 8: GLADIĀTŌRĒS

BRIEF OUTLINE

Reading passages ⎫
Background material ⎰ gladiatorial shows

Chief grammatical points   accusative plural
                            superlative

NARRATIVE POINTS

Date	*Setting*	*Characters Introduced*	*Story Line*
A.D. 59	Pompeii:	Senator Regulus	Regulus gives
(sic)	Amphitheater		show, which
			ends in a riot
			between
			Nucerians and
			Pompeians.

GRAMMATICAL POINTS

accusative plural
    e.g. *puellae iuvenēs salūtāvērunt.*
increased incidence of superlative adjective
    e.g. *Pompēiānī erant īrātissimī, quod Rēgulus spectāculum rīdiculum ēdēbat.*

No new SENTENCE PATTERNS in this stage.

Model Sentences

An exhibition of gladiators is announced. The people of Pompeii hurry to the amphitheater to see it.

The illustrations should provide sufficiently strong clues to the new grammatical feature here introduced. You should, however, postpone comments on the formation of accusative plurals until students have read aloud and translated the sentences. Younger students should read aloud and translate the sentences at least twice.

The following words are new: *spectāculum, nūntiābant, clausae, murmillōnēs, saepe, victōrēs.*

gladiātōrēs

The senator Regulus celebrates his birthday by presenting gladiatorial games in Pompeii. Citizens from Nuceria, which does not have an amphitheater, flock to Pompeii and, when the combat is announced, rush to the amphitheater in such numbers that many Pompeians cannot enter.

This and the next two stories are closely connected and are based on a historical riot that occurred at Pompeii in A.D. 59 between the Pompeians and the Nucerians, the people of Nuceria. Tacitus reports these events in *Annals* XIV.17.

If students read through the background material first, they will better grasp the situation and events described in the Latin passages. The sentences in all these stories are rather long because they are providing students with practice in clauses introduced by *quod, postquam* and *ubi.* Reassure students, especially in junior high school, if they are frightened by sentences that are longer than those they have seen previously. Allow them more time to explore sentences for meaning. Ask questions about entire sentences, e.g. "When did the Pompeians hurry as fast as they could to the amphitheater?" (lines 12–13). Read the Latin sentences aloud for the students, not too slowly, but bracket the subordinate clauses by appropriate pauses. For example, *Pompēiānī*—PAUSE—*postquam nūntiōs audīvērunt*—PAUSE—*ad amphitheātrum quam celerrimē contendērunt.*

in arēnā

The Pompeians cheer for one set of gladiators in the first contest; the Nucerians back another set, who are the winners. Regulus angers the Pompeians by ordering the death of the defeated gladiators.

The contest between the two *rētiāriī* and the two *murmillōnēs* is essentially one of strategy: the retiarii try to take advantage of their easier mobility; the murmillones, their heavier equipment. While students are reading this story for the first time, ask comprehension questions that draw their attention to the gladiators' tactical maneuvers: "Why do the retiarii at first avoid a fight? Are the Pompeians right when

they say the retiarii are *ignāvī*? Why does the first murmillo attack the
two retiarii on his own? Was this what the retiarii were hoping for?" and
so on. Later focus discussion on the reactions of the spectators: "Why
did the Pompeians want mercy for the murmillones? What made the
Nucerians demand their death? Why did Regulus side with the
Nucerians?" and so on.

First Language Note (Accusative Plural)

Follow up the language note in one of several ways. You might ask
students to pick examples of the accusative plural out of sentences in the
previous stories of Stage 8. With the help of the table in section 3 of this
note, students should provide the Latin for "lion," "slaves" etc. in
English sentences like "I killed a lion," "the slaves ran," etc. Once
students respond confidently to such a drill, ask them to provide the
Latin for the nominative or the accusative of "friend" or "merchants."
Unless the students are quite proficient, however, restrict the drill to the
English of nouns included in the table only. Do not outpace the
understanding of students. If the majority hesitate to answer or become
overly confused, postpone further integration of this new grammatical
point until students have had more experience reading Latin examples of
it.

vēnātiō

A wild animal fight staged in the amphitheater fails to appease the angry
spectators, and a bloody riot breaks out between the Nucerians and
Pompeians.

Balsdon, *Life* 308 distinguishes, besides the animal show, three
different kinds of spectacles with animals: armed men fighting animals,
animals pitted against other animals, and unarmed men and women
exposed to wild beasts. Students who remember their Sunday school
lessons may cite as an example of this last, third kind of animal spectacle
the martyrdom of Christians during the Roman persecution of A.D. 64.
In the present story, animals are matched against animals in a graded
sequence, with progressively more powerful beasts released into the
arena to fight and kill their predecessors. The same arrangement was
sometimes employed with only humans as combatants; each incoming
gladiator would be matched against the winner of the previous contest.

The students should not answer the comprehension questions printed
at the end of story until after they have read it in class with you.
Question 3, with its emphasis on the dissatisfaction that the Pompeians
felt with the first part of the show, might lead to further questions. "Why
did the Pompeians and Nucerians react differently to the first part of the

show?" (Regulus' refusal to commute death for the murmillones may be relevant here. Or the Pompeians might still have resented the Nucerians, in "gladiātōrēs," filling the larger part of the amphitheater.) Students might here read or reread the background material that describes the riot of A.D. 59.

pāstor et leō

This story, based on the well-known legend of Androcles and the lion, covers most of the grammatical points introduced previously, and is provided for review. Junior high school students love to act out this story, preferring usually to mime a parody of the action while a narrator reads the story. One student in a middle-school class we observed brought a large, stuffed lion whom she walked (limped?) through his paces.

The original version of the legend comes from Aulus Gellius, *Noctes Atticae* V.14.30. Older students may enjoy reading the play *Androcles and the Lion* by George Bernard Shaw.

Drills

Exercise 1   Type: completion
             Missing item: pronoun *or* noun *or* verb
             Test of accuracy: sense and pattern of sentence
             Grammatical points being practiced: structure of simple
                 sentences; 1st and 2nd persons singular of present tense,
                 introduced in Stage 4
             Grammatical point incidentally practiced: accusative plural

Exercise 2   Type: completion
             Missing item: verb
             Test of accuracy: correct personal ending
             Grammatical point being practiced: 1st, 2nd and 3rd
                 persons singular of present tense, introduced in Stage 4

Second Language Note (Superlative)

Although examples of the superlative have been appearing in the students' textbook ever since Stage 2, we have postponed the language note, in accordance with the principles of the course, until students have built up considerable experience in meeting superlatives. Consequently, you may follow up study of the note with a hunt for the superlatives in previous stories and stages. An excellent homework assignment, which doubles as review, is for students to write a list of all the Latin superlatives that appear in Stages 2–8, appending the numbers of the pages on which they appear.

The Background Material

For additional information about gladiatorial games, see Balsdon, *Life* 244–339, especially 288–313; Paoli 249–55; and Grant, *Gladiators*. Refer students, in their textbooks, to photographs on p. 120: Pompeiian wall painting of heavy-armed gladiators (one, perhaps wounded, is sitting on his shield, and the other is approaching for the kill); on p. 128: terracotta fragment (from the Museo Teatrale alla Scala, Milan) showing, in relief, *bēstiāriī* fighting (left to right) a female lion, a bear, and a male lion.

The drawing on page 130 is based on a wall-painting from Pompeii, reproduced on p. 124 of the students' textbook. It shows the entire amphitheater. At the back is the *vēlum*, attached to the town wall and ready to be drawn forward. This painting, probably the work of a Pompeian artist, shows the riot in progress, with groups fighting in the arena, on the seats and staircases, and in the area outside. Under the trees in the foreground are the stands of the food-venders, who, with the permission of the aediles, did business there, probably selling snacks and refreshments during the shows.

Another sketch, not shown in the textbook, depicts a gladiator descending a flight of steps and holding a palm-branch of victory proudly above his head; it may well refer to the same incident. Under it were scrawled the words, "*Campani, victoria una cum Nucerinis peristis*" ("Men of Campania, you died with the Nucerians in the same victory").

Reaction of students to the content of this stage ranges from blood-thirsty pleasure to disgust and criticism. Although students should express what they feel, you should also make sure that they see the games in their historical context as a social institution, which—whatever we think about it—was an extremely popular leisure occupation. Only afterwards should students draw parallels with particularly violent modern sports like international class boxing, Big Ten football, or Canadian ice hockey. (The status of a gladiator can also be compared with that of a modern sports star with a million-dollar contract.) Teachers ought not to endorse violence, but they also should not obscure the truth that violence has always exerted, and still exerts, a near-magnetic fascination.

Words and Phrases Checklist

Remind students again that, as stated on p. 51 above, *agitat*, or "chases" is related to *agit*, or "drives, acts." If they themselves do not notice, indicate to students that *gladius*, or "sword," is related to *gladiātor.* "Despite the etymology of their name, did all gladiators fight with swords?"

Suggestions for Further Work

1 Older high school, collegiate institute, or university students should, if time allows, present oral reports or write research papers on the four types of Roman gladiator: the murmillo, with a fish as his helmet crest, and the Samnite, with a square shield—both heavy-armed; the retiarius, with net and trident; and the Thracian, with round shield and crescent sword.

2 These same students, preferably after the above reports or research, might want to write a hypothetical "news dispatch" for a supposedly cross-time "wire service," in which a gladiatorial or animal game is described for modern newspaper readers. A dispassionate report about Androcles and the lion in the arena, written by a hypothetical reporter who did not know the background, would force the student writing it to review the Latin.

3 An incised shard (i.e. broken piece of pottery), now in the museum of Leicester, England, couples the name of an actress with that of a gladiator: "*Verecunda ludia [et] Lucius gladiator.*" Ask students to imagine the actress trying to persuade Lucius, before he became a gladiator, not to sign on and enter training at a gladiatorial school. "What might she have said to shake his resolve? Why might he have argued back?"

4 "A pair of murmillones is waiting in the tunnel just before going out into the arena to fight. They have been in training together, and are personal friends. What might they say to each other?" "If these two murmillones had been the same as the two in 'in arēnā,' who fought during the quarrel between the Pompeians and Nucerians, what might they have said while they waited to go into the arena, listening to the rioting above their heads?"

5 Show the first part of a videotape of the Hollywood costume epic *Spartacus*, 1960: Stanley Kubrick. Although this film is very long (190 minutes) and perhaps not worth showing in its entirety because of the romantic twaddle mixed with the patriotic fervor of the battle scenes, the opening phase of the film shows the basic training program in a gladiatorial school and an exciting gladiatorial duel.

STAGE 9: THERMAE

BRIEF OUTLINE

Reading passages ⎫ Background material ⎭	the baths
Chief grammatical point	dative singular and plural

NARRATIVE POINTS

Date	Setting	Characters Introduced	Story Line
A.D. 79	Pompeii: Palaestra	Milo (athlete)	Quintus' birthday visit to baths with Caecilius. Milo hurls discus; Quintus then hurls it and damages Milo's statue.
	Pompeii: Forum store	Marcellus (merchant)	Metella and Melissa buy Quintus a new toga for his birthday.
	Pompeii: Baths	Sceledrus and Anthrax (public slaves), anonymous thief	Sceledrus and Anthrax catch a toga-thief.

GRAMMATICAL POINTS

dative singular and plural

e.g. *mercātor fēminīs togās ostendit.*

ego, tū: nominative, accusative, & dative

e.g. *ego tibi grātiās maximās agō.*

reduplicated perfect

e.g. *Marcellus Metellae togam trādidit.*

sē

e.g. *āthlētae in palaestrā sē exercēbant.*

eō

e.g. *cīvēs cotīdiē ad thermās ībant.*

ferō

e.g. *servī oleum et strigilēs ferēbant.*

SENTENCE PATTERNS

NOM + DAT + ACC + V

e.g. *Quīntus servō pecūniam dedit.*

personal pronouns as subjects gradually suppressed

Model Sentences

Quintus celebrates his birthday.

Although dative forms now appear in the sentence pattern nominative + dative + accusative + verb, students will probably find little difficulty, especially if you encourage them to deduce the meaning of the Latin from the illustrations. Ask students questions about the pictures, and, with their answers, fix the three subplots in their mind—Quintus breaking off the statue's nose, Metella buying Quintus a birthday toga, and Quintus celebrating his birthday with a dinner—so that students can more readily distinguish the meaning of the new, dative inflections. "What is the small object in Quintus' right hand?" (Answer: a coin) "To whom is he giving it?" (Answer: to the man) "Good. So what does *servō* in 'Quintus gave the money *servō*' mean?" (Answer: to the slave) "Good. Melissa has a coin in her right hand. So what does *mercātōrī* in 'Melissa gave the money *mercātōrī*' mean?" (Answer: to the merchant) "Good. So what does *ancillae* in 'Quintus gave the signal *ancillae*' mean?" (Answer: to the slave-girl) "Good. In Latin, the whole sentence is *Quīntus ancillae signum dedit*. How do you think Quintus gave the signal to Melissa?" (Possible answers: He bit loudly into his fresh apple. Or he winked at her.)

With younger students, multiply and repeat questions, like the above, that relate the sentences to the pictures. With older students, after the first round of questions and the initial translation, design a structural chart on the blackboard:

"to (the) …"	"to (the) …"
Quīntus <u>servō</u> pecūniam dedit.	*Quīntus <u>amīcīs</u> discum ostendit.*
Melissa <u>mercātōrī</u> pecūniam dedit.	*mercātor <u>fēminīs</u> togās ostendit.*
Quīntus <u>ancillae</u> signum dedit.	*Clēmēns <u>hospitibus</u> vīnum offerēbat.*

"for (the/her/his) …"
Metella <u>fīliō</u> dōnum quaerēbat.
Metella <u>Quīntō</u> togam ēlēgit.
coquus <u>Quīntō</u> cēnam parābat.

The following words and phrases, in the model sentences, are new, though the pictures illustrate many of them: *ad thermās, discum novum, ferēbat, statuam, percussit, nāsum frāctum, dōnum, togās,* and *ēlēgit*. Some of the new words have obvious English derivatives that will help students fix the meanings of the Latin in their mind: "disc" (variant of "disk"); "statue"; "percussion" as in "percussion instrument" (= drum); "nasal"; "fracture"; "donation"; and "elect"; North American students tend to have a very loose notion of what a "toga" really was in antiquity. They are likely to associate "toga" with the sheet they drape around them at "Roman banquets" or amateur dramatic productions of the kind advocated in this Manual. The true toga was a draped, outer garment. It was generally made of wool and its shape was not rectangular but, rather, semicircular. It was restricted, at least in historical times, to men. Roman matrons wore the *stola*, a long outer garment that reached to their ankles (cf. the stola Metella wears in the pictures).

thermae

Pompeii's three bath-complexes are mentioned. Various activities associated with the baths are described, along with some parts of the bath-complex itself.

Very few datives appear in this story, but they become more frequent in the stories following.

To help students understand the technical terms—apodyterium, caldarium etc.— and the general social content of the Latin, begin with a preliminary discussion of the background material, where a ground plan of the Pompeii Forum Baths is printed, together with a description of the way the various rooms were used. These Forum Baths are the setting of the story.

The more vividly the students imagine the setting, the better they will understand the story. To build up the impression of noise and commotion, get students to recall the atmosphere of a modern swimming-pool, especially on a hot summer day, when people have ample leisure. Emphasize that actual bathing was only part of the total activities in the baths. Draw, as parallel, the Finnish sauna, miniature versions of which are common in the private homes of some Canadians and Americans. Another parallel—and in some ways better, because the gymnasia are attached to pools—is the YM- or YWCA, where many of the same students reading this course may spend their afternoons and Saturdays. In colleges and universities, the PE (Physical Education) building is often a complex of pools, ball courts, and rooms with weights, punching bags, and other exercise devices.

Explain any remaining details that students may find obscure, particularly the use of *oleum* as an equivalent of soap, and the *strigil* as an equivalent of the coarse towel. Refer students, in their textbook, to the photograph of strigils and oil pots on p. 137. Demonstrate the use of a strigil with a ruler. Junior high school students will all volunteer (one student, however, will be enough!) to lie on the teacher's desk, while another volunteer strigils with a ruler. Be sure to identify the volunteer strigiling as *servus*, and the strigilee as *dominus*. Remind students always of the sharp class distinctions of Roman society. Ask the volunteer whether strigiling would be so much fun, if he were forced by birth or bodily purchase to strigil his master everyday? Do not allow the answer to be a straight "No," since variables, like affection and the enjoyment of gathering with acquaintances and friends, would have lightened the burden of routine.

Illustrate the bather's progress through the baths by showing appropriate visual material. See photographs on p. 144 of students' textbook: apodyterium of the Stabian Baths (clothes were placed in the niches and guarded by slaves); on p. 132: caldarium of the Forum Baths; filmstrip 33; slides 57–58.

servī cīvibus discōs quaerēbant is sometimes translated "the slaves looked for the citizens' discuses." Indicate that this is close to the required sense, but it needs rephrasing. Compare the model sentence *Metella fīliō dōnum quaerēbat* on page 135.

in palaestrā

On his birthday, Quintus visits the baths with his father. The famous athlete, Milo, makes a magnificent throw with Quintus' new discus, but when Quintus tries it himself, his erratic throw strikes and damages a statue which happens to be that of Milo!

The comprehension questions at the end of this story draw students' attention to the character of the athlete Milo. Invite the class to speculate why the town officials had erected at the palaestra a statue in his honor. For example, during a sports meet between the Pompeians and Nucerians, Milo might have won the deciding round and become a hero overnight. Alternatively, he might have won a meet in Rome and brought fame to his hometown. Whatever the answer, be sure to make students aware that the personal fame of an athlete (or musician or poet) often rebounds upon the city of his origin. The theme of fame, personal and communal, is part of the larger theme of status. Encourage students to see beyond Milo, the fictional hero of a Latin story, to all heroes and heroines in all times and places.

This story (and the next one) are convenient for oral drill and review of the imperfect and perfect tenses. "Why did the slaves offer wine in the imperfect tense (*offerēbant*) to the spectators?" "Why did the slave who retrieved the discus offer it in the imperfect tense (*offerēbat*) to Milo, who had not thrown it?" (Answer: He refused to take it, because it was not his; the slave, who was evidently confused, kept trying to hand it to him.)

Refer students, in their textbook, to the photograph of the Pompeii palaestra on p. 139.

Language Note

In the sentence examples, the dative form is written second in the sentence so that students can learn what is, for the time being, more important than its position: the dative's range of inflections and meanings. The language note comments on the *function* of the dative by contrasting it with the nominative and accusative in the context of complete sentences. The *form* of the dative (singular and plural) is shown only in contrast with the nominative singular. Do not try to construct fuller paradigms for the 1st, 2nd, and 3rd declensions until after students are reasonably familiar, from their reading, with the uses and terminations of the dative. After the class has studied this note, drill the students orally, asking some to spot, or locate, datives in the preceding stories; others to translate again the entire sentence containing the dative. Such drill fixes in the students' minds the "to" and "for" uses of the dative.

in tabernā

Metella and Melissa go shopping in the forum for a birthday present for Quintus. After haggling with a merchant, they buy him a new toga.

As the students explore this story, perhaps translating parts, keep score on the board as the bargaining proceeds: put Marcellus' demands in one column, Melissa's counteroffers in another. Thus, students can keep tabs on both persons, while they work their way toward a compromise. Then ask, "Who makes the final decision to buy the toga? Why, if Melissa paid the merchant, did he hand the purchased toga to Metella? Why did Melissa do the actual negotiating?"

Drills

Exercise 1 Type: completion
Missing item: verb
Test of accuracy: sense
Grammatical point incidentally practiced: dative

Exercise 2 Type: completion
Missing item: verb
Test of accuracy: correct number of personal ending
Grammatical point being practiced: 3rd person singular and
plural of perfect, introduced in Stage 6
Grammatical point incidentally practiced: dative

Exercise 3 Type: completion
Missing item: verb *or* noun *or* prepositional phrase
Test of accuracy: sense, based on story "in tabernā"

in apodytēriō

This dramatic narrative recreates a theft in the apodyterium: the slaves Sceledrus and Anthrax apprehend a thief who is attempting to steal a rich man's toga.

The text of the story contains most of the inflections and sentence patterns that students have learned heretofore, including those new to this stage. A central issue in discussion might be the social status of the *fūr*. "Is the thief a slave or a freeborn man?" While deciding on the answer to this question, students should consider whether, if the thief were a slave, he would need to steal a toga or even, if he had been successful, he would have dared wear it in public. (Retort: He could have sold it, or perhaps he could have used the toga, made of wool, as a blanket for his sick wife.) If the thief were a slave, would not his owner have provided a doctor and medical care, like warm blankets? (Retort: Some slave-owners were notoriously stingy about providing medical services for their slaves.) If the thief were a slave, would not his owner have fed the ten, supposedly hungry, children? (Retort: If some owners stinted their payments for medical care, could they not also have stinted supplies of food?) If the thief were a *lībertus*, or "freedman," he could have been on his own, and not all freedmen were as successful as the *nouveau riche* Trimalchio, in Petronius' *Satyricon*. The true social status of the thief is implied in the final stage direction: he was brought before the judge. A slave would have been beaten by his master, who would himself have been legally liable for what his slave stole. But the real giveaway is in line 9, when the thief takes off his own toga. Only Roman citizens could wear the toga. The thief, therefore, must have been freeborn or a freedman.

The Background Material

For further information on the baths, see Balsdon, *Life* 26–32 and Paoli 221–27; on the baths at Pompeii, see Brion 120–28 and Maiuri 33–36.

Baths were built in growing numbers, both in Rome and in the Italian towns. In the time of Augustus, Rome had 170 public baths, and they continued to proliferate until, by the end of the Empire, the city may have had as many as 900 or more. At Pompeii there were three public baths. The oldest, called the Stabian Baths, and dating from the second century B.C., stand at the junction of the via di Stabia and the strada dell' Abbondanza. It is divided into two sections, for men and women respectively. It underwent progressive modernization until, in its final form, it was lavishly equipped and decorated, and had some of the finest examples known to us of Roman stucco decoration.

The Forum Baths are very well preserved in parts. They were built about 80 B.C., at the beginning of the period of Roman colonization, and, like the Stabian Baths, have separate accommodations for men and women.

The third bath complex at Pompeii, known as the Central Baths, is situated at the crossroads of the via de Nola and the via di Stabia. They formed part of the public works program after the earthquake of A.D. 62, and were designed on a grand scale with large, airy, well-lighted rooms; they were never finished.

The main hours for going to the baths were in the afternoon, but they were quite flexible. If no separate accommodations were available for women, they generally used the baths in the morning; elderly people also seem to have bathed in the morning. Most baths in the Italian towns, and many also in Rome, were run as commercial enterprises by private individuals who contracted the lease for a given period of time. The contractor, or Latin *conductor*, would appoint a baths superintendent, or *balneātor*, and charge an admission fee, usually quite small.

The purpose of these establishments was certainly not limited to a concern for personal hygiene. Bathing is a pleasurable and relaxing physical activity; the Romans enjoyed it all the more in the company of their fellows. The baths were an extremely popular and fashionable social meeting place. They were also regarded by some critics as an indication of social decadence on a par with extravagant dinner parties. Some certainly deserved a bad reputation, being little more than a cover for prostitution. But the majority contributed to public hygiene and to general social well-being. The uninhibited delight of the Pompeians in the pleasures of bathing, the chatter of friends, and the shouts of attendants and peddlers must have filled these barrel-vaulted rooms with an echoing din and much happy excitement.

Words and Phrases Checklist

Students may better remember *trādit*, or "hands over," if they remember that *-dit* is a variation on *dat*, "gives," and *trā-* is a shortened form of *trāns-*, "across": "gives across" becomes, more idiomatically, "hands over." If students ask, be prepared to explain why *fert* does not have a vowel before the personal ending *-t*. The verb is irregular, and the stem-vowel is missing also in *fers* and *fertis*, the second person forms. Finally, *suus* is strictly "his (own)" and may also mean "her (own)" and "its (own)," depending on the gender of the noun to which it refers. Students most easily learn *suus* as the third person form of *meus*, "my (own)," and *tuus*, "your (own)," and the gender of the person implied by the stems *me-*, *tu-*, *su-* ("I," "you," "she, he, it") depends on the gender of the noun to which the adjective refers. *Metella servō suō signum dedit* means "Metella gave the signal to *her* (own) slave"; *Caecilius servō suō signum dedit* means "Caecilius gave the signal to *his* (own) slave." The gender of the termination, here *-ō* in *suō*, is determined by the gender of the noun it modifies, here *servō*.

Suggestions for Further Work

1 "Draw a ground plan of a complex of Roman baths and label it. Add brief explanations of the labels."
2 "Imagine that you are an attendant at a Roman bath and that you are describing your job to a friend, while having a drink with him in the evening at an inn."
3 "Reread 'thermae.' Collect from the story all examples of *dominī* and of *servī*, then list in one column all the verbs after 'masters'; in another, all the verbs after 'slaves.' Do you notice any sharp contrast, between the lists, in the meanings of the verbs? Is there another noun in the story that is treated as the equivalent of *dominī*? What is it?" (Answer: *cīvēs*).

STAGE 10: RHĒTOR

BRIEF OUTLINE

Reading passages	education
Background material	
Chief grammatical points	1st and 2nd persons plural present comparative

NARRATIVE POINTS

Date	*Setting*	*Characters Introduced*	*Story Line*
A.D. 79	Pompeii: school	Theodorus (teacher), Alexander (friend of Quintus)	Debate: "Greeks are better than Romans"; Alexander wins: "Romans are imitators."
	Pompeii: Alexander's house	Diodorus and Thrasymachus (brothers of Alexander)	Quarrel over 3 gifts for Alexander's two brothers; Quintus settles it by taking one for himself.
	Pompeii: tavern		Syphax pays tavern bill with old Egyptian ring; bad luck comes to all. Grumio and Poppaea eventually find it. What happens to them?

GRAMMATICAL POINTS

1st and 2nd persons plural present (including *sum*)
    e.g. *nōs Graecī sumus sculptōrēs. nōs statuās pulchrās facimus.*
comparative adjective
comparison with *quam*
    e.g. *nōs sumus callidiōrēs quam vōs.*
nōbīs, vōbīs
    e.g. *nōs Rōmānī vōbīs pācem damus.*
questions with *-ne*
    e.g. *vōsne estis contentī?*
imperative, singular and plural
    e.g. *dā mihi statuās! abīte!*
in + accusative
    e.g. *Thrasymachus librum in piscīnam dēiēcit, quod īrātissimus erat.*

SENTENCE PATTERN

NOM + DAT *et* DAT + ACC + V

    e.g. *Quīntus rhētorī et amīcīs argūmentum explicāvit.*

Model Sentences

Inform students that the model sentences represent a debate between an imaginary *Rōmānus* and a *Graecus* who are debating the merits of their respective cultures. For the first reading aloud, choose two students to impersonate the debaters. The class should simulate a large jury and respond to the arguments, while each of the "debaters" advances, point by point, his case. Students are more likely to absorb the forms and meanings of the new personal endings if they themselves are absorbed in the cultural dispute behind the Latin sentences. Students unacquainted with French or Spanish may need help with *nōs* and *vōs*. Try not to tell them the meanings outright. Draw their attention to *Rōmānus dīcit* and *Graecus dīcit* and point out that these individuals, when they are quoted, are imagined as identifying with their tradition and establishing a contrast between their own people and the people of the opponent.

Among younger students, the "debaters" should stand at the front of the room, facing each other, and thereby illustrate face-to-face the "we–you" confrontation.

The pictures contain a large amount of detail. Students, after the first reading, should discuss them. You might invite intelligent speculation by asking questions. "Why did the Roman road surveyors and the Greek sculpture-copyists both use plumb-lines?" (Answer: In order to take bearings on a system of squares, so that workers would know where to cut the foundation trenches of roads; copyists, the marble. The Romans called this surveying instrument with plumb-lines hanging from crossbars, themselves set atop a bracket, a *grōma*, a word said to be related to Greek *gnōmon*, or "sundial pointer." If students wish to know how the groma works, there is a diagram in Hamey 22 and a longer discussion in Dilke, *Surveyors* 66–70). "Does anyone recognize the famous statue that the Greek craftsmen are copying?" (Answer: The Doryphoros, or "Spear-Bearer," originally by Polykleitos, a fifth-century B.C. Greek sculptor. The most perfect copy yet found of this statue came from the Samnite Palaestra at Pompeii. It was over-life-size, as in the illustration of the students' textbook.)

The model sentences draw a contrast between Greek intellectual and artistic skills, and Roman practicality. Ask younger students, in order to help them see the antithesis, "Is there any difference in the *sort* of things that the two nations are proud of?"

The photograph on p. 156 of the Roman bridge at Alcantara (Spain) is another example of Roman practical skills.

The following words are new: *architectī, pontēs, aedificāmus, fundōs, sculptōrēs, barbarī, ūtilēs,* and *quam* (= than).

contrōversia

This story recreates the debate of the model sentences in more elaborate and dramatic form. Theodorus sets the topic for the debate: *Graecī sunt meliōrēs quam Rōmānī.* Quintus speaks for Roman superiority and earns loud applause from the other Pompeian students. Alexander replies and, in the opinion of the rhetor, carries off the prize. Although the arguments are presented in fairly concrete terms, make sure that students understand the somewhat abstract *Graeciōrēs quam nōs Graecī.* "In what sense could the Romans have been more Greek than the Greeks?" (Possible answer: Because they took Greek literature and artifacts less for granted than did many Greeks, they would have noticed and talked about them more. Contrast the possible attitudes towards the Parthenon of modern Athenians who live within daily view of the Acropolis and North Americans who visit reconstructions of it at the Royal Ontario Museum, Toronto, or in a park of Nashville, Tennessee.)

Because this dramatic narrative has little action, you should bring out, during discussion, the disparity between the strong, loud emotions felt by the patriotic Roman students and the quiet decision in favor of the Greeks by the equally nationalistic Greek rhetor Theodorus. The verbal exchange is not just a school exercise on a well-worn theme. It raises old feelings of antagonism that resonated in the history of Pompeii itself, a city that had long maintained commercial links to the Greek world.

If time allows, use this story as an occasion to discuss briefly the development of the Roman *imperium* from the single town—later city—of Rome, to the cosmopolitan empire that comprised all the Mediterranean world. Or name and describe some *Graecī auctōrēs* and their *librī*; or show plates in art-books of *Graecae statuae*, beginning with the Doryphoros of Polykleitos.

Some Suggested Questions

"Why did the rhetor's class applaud Quintus?"
"Why was it Alexander who replied to Quintus?"
"Do you agree with Theodorus' final verdict? Was the rhetor's decision based on logical or emotional factors?"
"Can you say, in as few words as possible, the three ways in which, according to Quintus, the Romans are superior to the Greeks?" For this

last question, allow students, if necessary, to consult their textbooks; the value of the question lies in the review of Latin meanings that it encourages. Comprehension questions can be just as effective as word-for-word translation in assessing students' understanding of Latin.

statuae

This story describes an argument of a more elementary kind. Quintus acts as peacemaker when a quarrel breaks out between Alexander's two younger brothers, both of whom want the gift-statuette of a girl. He takes the opportunity to score a debating point over Alexander. Thrasymachus, however, has the last word.

Read the story aloud, expressively, and as rapidly as you can without the students' withdrawing their attention because they cannot understand at least the main line of the plot. Make clear, by tone of voice, the contrast between the peevishness of the small boys and the more grown-up behavior of the others. Quintus may be a bit superior-acting or self-important. If you ask students whether their own younger brothers behave like Thrasymachus and Diodorus, they will invariably reply "yes."

The separate pronouns *nōs* and *vōs*, here used as markers, will gradually be dropped, but as with *ego* and *tū*, they should, with junior high school students, be considered, as in English, parts of the verbs. Older students should ignore them as much as possible; to make certain that older students *are ignoring* the separate pronouns and looking at verb-endings to determine person, drill them orally with single verb-forms from the story. "What does *estis* (or *damus* or *accipitis*) mean?" Such drill will also eventually be appropriate for younger students.

First Language Note (1st and 2nd Persons Plural)

As in the corresponding language note in Stage 4, where singular personal endings were summarized, you should follow up study of this note with further oral drill of the 1st and 2nd persons plural forms of verbs included among the previous checklists (consult Cumulated List on pp. 114–16 below). To older students, give verbs without separate pronouns (e.g. *agitāmus* (Stage 8), *habēmus* (4), *cōnsūmitis* (8), *facitis* (7), and *dormītis* (2)) and ask a volunteer to repeat the verb in Latin and then translate it. For younger students, if necessary, add at first separate pronouns (e.g. *nōs agitāmus*), later omit these (e.g. *agitāmus*), but always proceed as suggested, asking volunteers to repeat the Latin form after you and then to translate it. (You will assure closer attention if you ask students to answer, but do not name a particular student until after you have pronounced the Latin form.)

When most students seem secure in their knowledge of these new personal endings, extend the oral translation drill to include all persons of the verbs previously drilled (e.g. *agitat, habent, cōnsūmō, facis,* and *dormiunt*). If students are unsure of endings, add separate pronouns or nouns (e.g. *dominus agitat*), but later, when the students are more secure in their knowledge, drop pronouns or nouns and return to single verb-forms. In college or university classes, after rapid and full oral drill of all the persons of many different checklist verbs, organize the information on the blackboard, writing all the persons, singular and plural, of selected verbs. We recommend one example of each conjugation (including "-iō" forms of the third): *agitō, habeō, cōnsūmō (faciō),* and *dormiō*. Students may themselves cite the correct forms in order, while you write on the board; or individual students may go to the board and write them. You should provide Latin examples of each of the conjugations, not expect students to retrieve them, at this point, from their memory. It is more important now to drill endings within the conjugations, not to scrutinize ability in distinguishing among conjugations.

Verbs listed in the checklists of Stages 1–9 may be organized as follows:

1st			2nd
agitāre (8)	incitāre (8)	pugnāre (8)	exercēre (9)
ambulāre (5)	intrāre (2)	pulsāre (6)	habēre (4)
celebrāre (9)	labōrāre (1)	rogāre (7)	manēre (9)
cēnāre (7)	lacrimāre (7)	salūtāre (2)	respondēre (3)
circumspectāre (3)	laudāre (2)	spectāre (5)	rīdēre (3)
clāmāre (3)	nārrāre (7)	stāre (5)	sedēre (1)
exspectāre (3)	necāre (7)	superāre (6)	terrēre (7)
festīnāre (6)	parāre (7)	vituperāre (6)	vidēre (3)
gustāre (2)	portāre (3)	vocāre (4)	
habitāre (8)	postulāre (8)		

3rd		3rd "-iō"	4th
agere (4)	ostendere (9)	cōnspicere (7)	audīre (5)
agnōscere (9)	petere (5)	cupere (9)	dormīre (2)
bibere (3)	plaudere (5)	facere (7)	revenīre (9)
cōnsūmere (8)	prōcēdere (7)	īnspicere (9)	venīre (5)
contendere (5)	quaerere (4)		
coquere (4)	recumbere (8)		
currere (5)	reddere (4)		
dūcere (8)	scrībere (6)		
emere (6)	surgere (3)		
ēmittere (9)	trādere (9)		
intellegere (7)	vēndere (4)		

The verbs in the lists above and in Appendix A on pp. 114–16 below are given in their infinitive forms, not for the students (who have not yet seen infinitive forms), but for the teacher, who will find them convenient for finding the stem (drop final -*re*) of each verb. (Verbs here and in Appendix A are also shown in their infinitive form for consistency with corresponding lists in Manuals to later Units.) Periodically, in those last few minutes of class when there is not time to begin a new story or lengthy drill, you might drill the meanings of a few verb stems alone. For example, "What does *pugnā*- mean?" (Answer: fight) "What does *pugnāmus* mean?" (Answer: we fight) "What does *ostende*- mean?" (Answer: show) "What does *ostenditis* mean?" (Answer: you (pl.) show) And so forth. This kind of drill is extremely effective as review of dictionary meanings, as well as personal endings. If you give students examples from groups of verbs *within* a conjugation, students will subconsciously learn to distinguish conjugations with minimal pain. Irregular verbs like *esse* and its compounds *adesse* and *abesse*, *īre* and its compound *abīre*, and *ferre* should be drilled separately from more regular forms like those in the lists above.

ānulus Aegyptius

This story deals with the familiar theme of a magic ring and the consequences of owning it. The scene is a tavern, where Syphax, short of money, pays his bill with an ancient Egyptian ring. Bad luck then plagues the tavern-owner, his wife, and finally, a slave who steals the ring from them. Grumio, out for a walk with Poppaea, finds the ring. Poppaea thinks it will bring them good luck. Will it?

The narrative contains many sentences with dative forms. After exploring the story and asking comprehension questions and/or assigning translations of selected phrases or sentences, ask students to spot, or pick out, the datives and translate them. Most examples of the inflection can be translated with English "to" (e.g. *Syphācī* as "to Syphax"). The possible exception is *caupōnī* in *Syphāx caupōnī respondit* (line 7: "Syphax answered the innkeeper"). Although a student may "correct" the translation by suggesting "Syphax replied to the innkeeper," you should stress that "answered the innkeeper" is also correct, since the phrase carries the same meanings as "replied to the innkeeper" and is considerably more idiomatic.

Note also that from now on *est* is moved frequently to a final position, for example *ānulus antīquus est*. This relaxation of word order (*est* in the middle or at the end of the sentence) becomes normal in subsequent stages.

During a second reading aloud, you may punctuate your reading with English comprehension questions. At appropriate moments, you should ask "Who has the ring now?" Students enjoy solving this kind of puzzle, and they review the Latin while looking for the answers. Other comprehension questions appear in the students' textbook.

Drills

Exercise 1 Type: completion
Missing item: accusative + verb
Test of accuracy: sense
Grammatical point incidentally practiced: 1st person plural present

Exercise 2 Type: completion
Missing item: noun
Test of accuracy: sense
Grammatical point incidentally practiced: 1st and 2nd persons plural present

While working with this stage, you should review the dative with students. You might ask them to pick out examples of the dative in sentences from "ānulus Aegyptius" (adding a translation of the sentence) or to say which word, in an English sentence made up by you, would be translated by a nominative/accusative/dative.

As the class approaches the last two stages of Unit 1, begin consolidation of grammar by working in class or assigning as homework some appropriate paragraphs in the Review Grammar part of the Language Information Section (pp. 202–12 of the students' textbook). See pp. 105–109 below for suggestions for presenting this material.

Second Language Note

Because the students have now met several examples of the comparative adjective, particularly in this stage, they should study the note carefully so that they can integrate their knowledge of the separate examples. If students seem unsure of their knowledge, go back with them through this stage and spot examples of comparatives: e.g. *nōs sumus callidiōrēs quam vōs* in the model sentences, or *urbs Rōma est maior quam omnēs urbēs* in "contrōversia" (line 19). Assign to younger students, as homework, a treasure-hunt for comparatives. Ask them to find, copy out, and translate all sentences in Stage 10 that contain comparatives. Award extra credit to students who find examples in previous stages.

The Background Material

An excellent recent account of Roman education is given by Bonner. See also Marrou and Barrow. Shorter discussions are given by Paoli 167–73, and Balsdon, *Life* 92–106.

Suggestions for Discussion

1 " What are the most obvious differences between ancient Roman and modern American (or Canadian) schools? What similarities do you notice?"

2 "How is the curriculum in North American elementary schools similar to that of classes taught by the *lūdī magister*? How is the curriculum in North American high schools or collegiate institutes similar to that of classes taught by the *grammaticus*? How do the curricula now differ? Why do they differ?"

3 " Would you have preferred going to school in Pompeii to going to school where you do? Explain."

Words and Phrases Checklist

Our experience indicates that students tend to remember *servat*, or "saves," incorrectly as "serves" (= Latin *servit*). If necessary, you should teach them a mnemonic device, like "*servat* and *saves* both have 'a's.'"

STAGE 11: CANDIDĀTĪ

BRIEF OUTLINE

Reading passages ⎱
Background material ⎰ elections

Chief grammatical points *faveō, crēdō,* and *placet* with dative
direct questions

NARRATIVE POINTS

Date	Setting	Characters Introduced	Story Line
March A.D. 79	Pompeii: house of Marcus and Quartus	Marcus and Quartus (brothers), Sulla (sign-painter), Holconius and Afer (candidates)	Sulla makes a profit by painting signs for brothers advertising their candidates.
	Near the Amphitheater		Grumio tries to earn money by voting illegally.
	Forum		Clemens earns 10 denarii by rescuing Caecilius from riot
	Caecilius' house		Clemens goes out with Poppaea.

intransitive verbs (*crēdō, faveō, placet*) + dative
   e.g. *nōs mercātōrī favēmus.*
placet
   e.g. *mihi placet.*
increased incidence of questions with *quis, quid,* etc. with no interrogative
    word, with *num,* with *-ne*
   e.g. *quō festīnās, Grumiō? num tū Āfrō favēs?*
increased incidence of imperative vocative
   e.g. *Marce! Quārte! dēsistite! intrō īte!*
mēcum, tēcum
   e.g. *tū mēcum venīs?*
sibi
   e.g. *Quārtus sibi dīxit, "frāter meus est stultissimus."*

SENTENCE PATTERN
NOM + DAT + V
   e.g. *nōs candidātō nostrō nōn crēdimus sed favēmus.*

Model Sentences

Groups of Pompeians—farmers, merchants, bakers, young men, and
even thieves—express their views on the candidates they support. Dative
forms are here presented in two new contexts:

1 with a verb of replying, e.g. *mercātōrēs agricolīs respondent* and, in the
    reading passages, e.g. *Marcus Quārtō dīxit.* One example of this new
    usage appeared in Stage 10, in "ānulus Aegyptius." See comments on
    p. 86 above.
2 with two new verbs *faveō* and *crēdō.* For example, *nōs Lūciō favēmus,* and
    nōs āthlētae crēdimus.

The context and the accompanying pictures provide numerous clues to
the meaning of these new dative usages. Accept translations either with
or without English prepositions: "We support Lucius" and "We give our
support to Lucius" are both acceptable. If a student asks, say, why
"merchant" is not in the accusative in *nōs mercātōrī favēmus,* suggest that
favēmus corresponds to the English "We give our support ... " and then
ask how the English sentence should be finished. (Answer: to the
merchant) If students do not themselves raise the matter, however,
postpone discussion about diverging word patterns until after students
have studied the language note.

The following words are new: *candidātōs, noster, favēmus,* and *crēdimus.*

Marcus et Quārtus

The two brothers disagree sharply about who is the best candidate. Marcus supports Afer because he is a wealthy property owner, while Quartus favors Holconius because the family has held high office before. (In actual history, the Holconii had a long record of public service, including, for example, the renovation of Pompeii's theater.) This story, like the next one, is suitable, after the first reading, for dramatic reading or production. The production need not be elaborate. Students may walk through their parts, holding their books, and the student-*scrīptor* Sulla may write his *titulī* on the blackboard with colored chalk. Because the brothers Marcus and Quartus are, like many persons in electorates everywhere, enthusiastic boosters of their candidates, actors should exaggerate in their dramatization the imperatives and superlatives (e.g. "est candidatus OPPPP-ti-mus").

The new expressions *mihi placet* and *tibi placet* are also introduced in this story. In these impersonal expressions, the dative is placed directly before the verb (whereas in sentences with accusatives, the datives were placed before these nouns, e.g. "*servō* ānulum trādidit"). You should, however, encourage a variety of suitable translations. For example,

placetne tibi?—"Does that suit you?"
"Is that all right (slang: 'OK') for you?"
"Will that do for you?"

Students will better visualize the sign-painter at work, if they study the illustration on p. 181 of their textbook. (This particular sign-painter, unlike the Sulla of the story, is working by night and therefore needs the lamps above his shoulder.)

Sulla

Marcus and Quartus, by turns, engage a sign-painter, Sulla, to paint slogans advertising their favorite candidates. When, finally, the two brothers come to blows, Sulla settles the dispute (and makes a handsome profit) by painting a sign for each of them.

Some Suggested Questions

Why was Marcus angry (line 2)?
Was the slogan *Marcus et frāter Āfrō favent* (lines 11–12) completely true?
Why does Marcus want the words *et frāter* included?
How much money, including the money paid in the previous story, did the sign-painter Sulla receive from the brothers altogether?

Lūcius Spurius Pompōniānus

In these four episodes, the slave Grumio tries to pass for a citizen with normal voting rights. The boisterous character of these short dramatic pieces has made them favorites among classroom actors, especially junior high schoolers. Simultaneously with the excitement, these dramatic scenes provide students with review of grammatical points so far introduced, particularly of the present tense (all persons, singular and plural) and of the accusative and dative cases.

in vīllā

Grumio describes to Clemens his scheme to pose as a citizen of Pompeii, Lucius Spurius Pomponianus (a baker), in order to get the five denarii which Afer has promised his supporters in the election. Clemens, concerned for Grumio's safety, decides to accompany him to the rally near the amphitheater.

Some Suggested Questions

Why does Clemens think Grumio ought to support Holconius?
Why does Grumio in fact support Afer?
When Grumio calls himself Lucius Spurius Pomponianus, why does he give himself three names?
Why does Clemens describe Grumio's plan as *perīculōsam* (line 21)?
Is direct payment to the electorate the only form of political bribery? Can you suggest some indirect forms of bribery that dishonest politicans might practice?

prope amphitheātrum

At the rally, Grumio receives the expected handout, but he is also given a club, which puzzles him. Clemens puts in a sarcastic remark about Afer's generosity, and then Afer himself arrives.

Some Suggested Questions

On which word in Grumio's speech *salvē . . . sumus* (lines 4–6) does he hit Clemens?
Why does Grumio describe himself and Afer as *amīcissimī?*
What does Grumio receive from the *dīvīsor* besides the denarii? Why?

in forō

Grumio and Clemens, along with a group of bakers, accompany Afer to the forum, where Clemens spots Caecilius among Holconius' contingent. Grumio flees in confusion, and there follows a scuffle between Afer's supporters and the merchants, who favor Holconius.

Some Suggested Questions

How does Grumio's tone of voice change during his speech *euge! fēminās ...! ... ad vīllam reveniō!* (lines 7–9)?

Can you suggest some possible reasons why Caecilius was a supporter of Holconius?

in culīnā

Clemens is in the kitchen when Grumio arrives, looking much the worse for wear. Grumio has gotten mixed up in the riot and lost his money, while Clemens, for rescuing Caecilius from the same riot, has received ten denarii from his master. What is more, to Grumio's embarrassment, Clemens has a date with Poppaea.

Some Suggested Questions

What happened to Grumio's toga?

Why do you think the merchants described Grumio as being *fortis* when they saw him in the forum?

Why do you think Poppaea has apparently switched her affection from Grumio to Clemens?

Do you feel sorry for Grumio at the end of this play? Or do you believe he got what was coming to him?

You might, at the conclusion of the episodes, give the result of historical elections to the Pompeian duovirate in A.D. 79. The winning candidates were M. Holconius Priscus and C. Cerrinus Vatia.

The episodes of the Pomponianus-play provide students with an opportunity to review all the persons, singular and plural, of the present tense. Provide further oral drill by asking students to translate variations on verb-forms appearing in the text: "What does *videō* in line 6 (in 'in forō') mean? What would *vidēmus* have meant? What would *vident* have meant?" And so forth.

First Language Note (faveō etc. with Dative)

After students have studied the language note, drill them further by asking them to translate examples taken from passages in this stage. Then, contrast the sentence patterns with which students are by now familiar. Write on the blackboard a sentence of the nominative + dative + verb pattern like *cīvēs Holcōniō favent*, and under this write a sentence of the nominative + accusative + verb pattern like *cīvēs Holcōnium salūtant*. Ask volunteers to translate the sentences, and then write the best translations under each. Finally, ask students to describe the differences between the two sentence patterns in their own words.

Drills

Exercise 1   Type: completion
              Missing item: verb
              Test of accuracy: sense and correct personal endings
              Grammatical point being practiced: 1st and 2nd persons
                  singular and plural of present tense, introduced in Stage
                  10

Exercise 2   Type: completion
              Missing item: noun
              Test of accuracy: correct inflection
              Grammatical point being practiced: nominative and
                  accusative singular, introduced in Stage 2; nominative
                  singular and plural, introduced in Stage 5; nominative
                  and accusative plural, introduced in Stages 5 and 8

Second Language Note (Types of Question)

Here we have gathered together examples of the various types of question that students have met so far. You might add practice examples to those included in the note by scouring the passages in previous stages. With young or less able older students, assign, as homework, another treasure-hunt like those previously recommended, and ask students to find and write out as many Latin questions as they can find.

   num-questions have been included in the reading material and in this note, but not *nōnne*-questions, which are not discussed until Stage 15. *num* ...? and *nōnne* ...? can be a bit tricky for students of any age to grasp; they are especially likely to confuse if presented to students simultaneously. Do not mention *nōnne* ...? at this point, unless students (usually transfers from other schools where they studied Latin from another textbook) bring it up themselves. If students should ask whether there is a word in Latin that suggests the answer "yes," tell them that the word is *nōnne . . . ?*, give them an example to translate, but then drop the matter and let your main emphasis fall on *num . . . ?* During translation drills, encourage students to use varied and idiomatic versions (e.g. "You don't mean to tell me that Grumio is working?" for *num Grumiō labōrat?*). Demonstrate to students that negative answers can be implied by tone of voice (e.g. *NUM* [emphatic, as though it were English "don't"] *vīnum bibis?*).

The Background Material

Local government in Pompeii was based on elective offices, and the competition for these was lively. The bureaucracy of the Empire, which later had a crushing effect on local political life, had not yet depressed it at Pompeii. Interestingly, the liveliest campaigning was for the aedileship, since election to the duovirate followed more or less automatically after holding the lower office.

If a magistrate had been successful at the polls in March, he took office in July. Thus, at the time of the eruption in A.D. 79, the duoviri had been in office for barely a month and the town was still "plastered" with electoral propaganda.

The wall inscriptions in the picture on page 181 of the students' textbook are copied from actual inscriptions that were discovered on the wall of the house of Trebius Valens. The unabbreviated forms and translations of the inscriptions are as follows:

top left	*Gaium Iulium Polybium aedilem viis aedibus sacris publicis procurandis*
	(Vote for) Gaius Iulius Polybius as aedile for supervising roads, sacred temples, and public works
top right	*Decimi Lucreti Satri Valentis flaminis gladiatorum paria decem pugnabunt*
	10 pairs of gladiators owned by Decimus Lucretius Satrius Valens, priest, will fight (Valens was a priest in the cult of Nero.)
middle left	*Marcum Holconium duovirum iure dicundo dignum re publica oramus vos faciatis*
	We beg you to make Marcus Holconius duovir for the administration of justice; he is worthy of public office
middle right	*lanternari tene scalam*
	Hold on to the ladder, lantern-bearer
bottom left	*Gnaeum Helvium Sabinum aedilem oramus faciatis*
	Lucium Ceium Secundum duovirum oramus faciatis
	We beg you to make Gnaeus Helvius Sabinus aedile
	We beg you to make Lucius Ceius Secundus duovir

bottom right   *Quintum Postumium Modestum*
                   (Vote for) Quintus Postumius Modestus

Supporters of a candidate usually based their campaign, not on political policy—since the scope for that, under the emperors, was limited—but rather on the candidate's character. The campaign slogan was usually worded as a simple formula. Here are some examples (*o.v.f.* is an abbreviation of *oramus vos faciatis*):

A. Vettium Firmum aed. o.v.f. dign. est.
Caprasia cum Nymphio rog.
We urge you to make A. Vettius Firmus aedile. He is worthy.
Caprasia asks this with Nymphius.

vicini often appear as the sponsors (*Q.P.P.* is an abbreviation of *Quintus Postumius Proculus*):

Q.P.P. aed. o.v.f. rogant vicini.
The neighbors urge you to make Quintus Postumius Proculus aedile.

Several campaign signs urge sponsors or candidates to wake up and act more energetically:

Trebi, surge, fac Helvium Sabinum aed., dormis.
Trebius, wake up (and) make Helvius Sabinus aedile; you are asleep.

In one instance, the sign alludes to the candidate's policy:

hic aerarium conservabit.
This candidate will watch the treasury.

Another good example represents the people who lived near the Porta Urbulana at the east end of town (*d.r.p.* is an abbreviation of *dignum re publica*):

L. Ceium Secundum II vir o.v.f. d.r.p. Urbulanenses rog.
The people (living by the) Porta Urbulana urge you to make Lucius Ceius Secundus duumvir. He is worthy of the common good.

Other groups who supported candidates were *mūliōnēs* (mule drivers), *sagāriī* (cloak-cutters), *saccāriī* (porters), *fullōnēs* (fullers), *piscicapī* (fishermen), and many others.

Some of these graffiti appear to have been put up with humorous intentions and occasionally, perhaps, to discredit the candidate. A group of chess-players, or *latrunculāriī*, decided to support the campaign of Montanus on behalf of his patron Lucius Popidius. Elsewhere, *dormientēs ūniversī*, or "all the sleepy-heads," back the unlucky Vatia. But politeness or bargaining is the more common rule:

Sabinu[m] aed. Procule fac et ille te faciet.
Proculus, make Sabinus an aedile, and he will make you (aedile).

The notices that skilled sign-painters put up were intended to be seen clearly from a distance. Their letters, painted in red, were often a foot high. Sometimes the sign-painter himself affixed his name. We find *scripsit Protogenes*, or "Protogenes wrote (this)," *Scr. Infantio cum Floro et Fructo et Sabino hic et ubique*, or "Infantio, (along) with Florus and Fructus and Sabinus, wrote (this) here and everywhere."

Finally, as one wise-cracker put it when he scrutinized the numerous writings on the wall:

admiror, paries, te non cecidisse ruinis,
   qui tot scriptorum taedia sustineas. (an elegiac couplet)
I am surprised, wall, that you have not fallen in ruins,
   (you) who bear up under so many boring signs.

We have followed the interpretation of some scholars of the wall-painting on p. 168 of the students' textbook, that it shows a free distribution of bread to bribe voters. The candidate need not have been a baker, but it is interesting that the name of one baker who held office as aedile is known, Paquius Proculus, part of whose tablinum is shown on p. 16. Other scholars think this painting shows a baker's store or maybe a charitable distribution.

Suggestions for Discussion

1 Help the class to decipher and interpret the slogans painted on the wall picture on p. 181 of their textbook. Students may want to copy some of the slogans from the picture or from the additional list above in this Manual onto the blackboard. If local elections are in full swing, students will want also to copy slogans from current posters or television advertisements and compare them with slogans from ancient Pompeii.

2 Invite students to comment on the process of electioneering described in this stage. Help them draw parallels and contrasts with local politics in their own town today. Who are their local officials? How often are they elected? How do the candidates gather support and campaign funds? What does a member of the town board, council, or selectmen do? What does the mayor or town manager do? And so forth.

Words and Phrases Checklist

Younger or less able students easily confuse *verberat*, or "strikes, beats," with *vituperat* (Stage 6), or "finds fault with, tells off, scolds." *verberat,* which can also mean "flogs, switches," is related to the word *verbēnae*, or "sacred branches." In North America, the "verbena" bush is well known for its vari-colored flowers. A different plant, with a name of the same etymology, called in France *vervain*, is common as a scent in toilet waters and colognes. *vituperat* is thought to have been compounded from *vitium* + *parāre*, or "lays on a fault," or "finds fault with."

Suggestions for Further Work

1 "Write and deliver an imaginary speech, in English, by a Pompeian candidate for the aedileship in the forum. Don't forget his promises to various power groups like the merchants and bakers. Include a few Latin sentences, if possible."
2 "Write a short story, recreating characters and the events leading up to the painted warning, mentioned above, 'Trebius, wake up (and) make Helvius Sabinus aedile; you are asleep.' What might the relationship between Trebius and Sabinus have been? Had Trebius loaned Sabinus money? Was he a neighbor? Did he practice the same profession? Why might he have been so powerful that he could influence the election of his friend? Why might Trebius have neglected to campaign for Sabinus?"
3 Junior high and high school students enjoy writing in Latin on posters their own campaign slogans for school elections, either actual or imaginary. You should help with vocabulary, cheerfully recognizing that at this point enthusiasm may outstrip expertise. Encourage students to use the abbreviation *o.v.f.* (= *ōrō vōs faciātis*) and add their name in English and as predicate the accusative of the Latin title. For example, *o.v.f.* Susan *Imperātrīcem* or *o.v.f.* Tom *Imperātōrem / Duumvirum / Aedīlem*.

STAGE 12: MŌNS VESUVIUS

BRIEF OUTLINE

Reading passages } Background material }	the eruption of Vesuvius, August 24, A.D. 79
Chief grammatical point	1st and 2nd persons singular and plural, imperfect and perfect.

NARRATIVE POINTS

Date	Setting	Characters Introduced	Story Line
August 24, A.D. 79	Pompeii: day of eruption	Julius (friend of Caecilius)	Turmoil: Clemens saves Julius, who then flees. Clemens finds Caecilius dying. Caecilius orders Clemens to find Quintus and give him Caecilius' signet ring. Caecilius dies, Clemens departs, Cerberus stands guard.

GRAMMATICAL POINTS

1st and 2nd persons singular and plural, imperfect and perfect
    e.g. *tū sonōs audīvistī. ego tremōrēs sēnsī.*
1st and 2nd persons singular and plural imperfect of *sum*
    e.g. *sollicitī erant.*
ablative plural in prepositional phrases
    e.g. *fēminae cum īnfantibus per urbem festīnābant.*

SENTENCE PATTERN

expansion of the subordinate clauses to contain DAT + ACC + V
    e.g. *Caecilius, postquam Clēmentī ānulum suum trādidit, statim exspīrāvit.*

Model Sentences

The citizens recognize the beginnings of the eruption.

    These sentences introduce into the sentence patterns the 1st and 2nd persons, singular and plural, of the imperfect and perfect tenses. Personal pronouns are used initially as markers, as they were with the present tense, and then gradually phased out. The new personal endings are worked into an aspect-contrasting format similar to that of the model sentences in Stage 6, where the imperfect and perfect tenses were shown, contrasted, side by side. The imperfect describes a continuous action (e.g. Syphax: "I was selling slaves"); the perfect indicates the intrusion of straightforward occurrence of an event (e.g. Syphax: "Suddenly I heard noises").

Notice that not all the first and second person forms of those tenses are represented in these model sentences. Do not expect students, at this point in their progress, to have a complete mastery of all the verb forms. The purpose of this part of the stage is to introduce endings and review the contrast between uses of the imperfect and perfect.

The following words are new: *sonōs, tremōrēs, sēnsī, nūbem, cinerem*, and *flammās*.

tremōrēs

This and all the stories remaining in Stage 12 present a connected description of the confusion that resulted from the eruption. Central to the narrative interest is the behavior and fate of Caecilius, his family, and his friends.

Caecilius is dining in the country with his friend Julius. They are discussing the recent tremors and the cloud over Vesuvius. Julius is worried, but Caecilius trusts in the gods, who saved him and his family in the earthquake some years before. They are startled by the appearance of Clemens, who is supposed to be visiting Caecilius' farm.

Some students become so engrossed as the sequence of events approaches its climax that they read very quickly to the end of the stage to find out what happens. On the first reading, you should allow them to do this, since the story is everything. You might encourage them to read rapidly by supplying, orally, forgotten meanings. Discussion of behavior and the general picture of fleeing families and falling buildings, and such questions as how many got away, where they went and so on, can wait for the second reading. Given the high level of interest, students learn the new inflections with relative ease.

Students will probably remember Nuceria (line 2; where Julius had his villa) from Stage 8 (in which Nucerians rioted at the amphitheater). For a contemporary description of the *nūbēs mīrābilis* (line 8), see Pliny, *Letters* VI.16.5–6, where the volcanic cloud is compared in shape to an Umbrella or Stone Pine (*Pinus Pinea*), the equivalent of the modern mushroom cloud associated with violent explosions like that of Mt. St. Helens, in southwestern Washington state, or atomic tests. (There is a drawing of the Umbrella Pine on Marx 6). Other students may remember the lararium of Caecilius from the discussion, Stage 1, about Caecilius' house. (The lararium is pictured in the illustration of the atrium, Stage 1, beside model sentence *Metella est in ātriō*; Stage 2, beside model sentence *Caecilius est in ātriō*.) Remind students that a Roman *familia* (line 11) was more extended than a North American family and included slaves. Remind them also that the reference in *iamprīdem terra tremuit* (line 16) is to the earthquake of A.D. 62 that was pictured on the two marble panels of Caecilius' actual lararium (see commentary on Stage 1, p. 24 of this Manual; also the additional notes on the background material in Stage 4, pp. 44–46 of this Manual).

ad urbem

Clemens explains that he and the farm manager fled to the city because they were frightened by the loud rumblings and clouds from the volcano. They found the city in turmoil, and Quintus sent Clemens to alert Caecilius, who now hurries to the city himself, along with Julius and Clemens. They encounter Holconius, who is fleeing the destruction. Questioning him, Caecilius is furious to find him too distracted by the loss of his own house and possessions to show any concern for Caecilius' family.

Some Suggested Questions

Caecilius supported Holconius in the elections described in Stage 11.
  Should Holconius have been more considerate of Caecilius' feelings when the latter asked him if he had seen his wife Metella?
Did Holconius answer Caecilius' questions: *tū Metellam vīdistī? Quintum cōnspexistī?* Why not?
Was Caecilius justified in insulting Holconius, or calling him *furcifer*?

ad vīllam

Caecilius, Julius, and Clemens fight the crowds in the streets, and presently Julius falls unconscious. Clemens carries him into a nearby temple of Isis, earning Caecilius' praise and a promise of freedom. Clemens remains with Julius as Caecilius presses on toward home, but follows his master as soon as Julius recovers.

Continue focusing students' attention on the story-line. Later, if there is time, they might discuss the actions and motives of the characters. "Why does Caecilius leave Clemens behind with Julius in the temple of Isis? Why does Julius call Caecilius *stultissimus?* Why does Julius leave the town? Where might Julius have gone? Why does Clemens follow Caecilius to his house?"

Note that, in lines 9–10, Caecilius promised to manumit (free from slavery) Clemens, in return for his carrying Julius to safety in the temple of Isis. Later, in Unit 2, Clemens, having become a *lībertus*, will establish himself as a glass-seller in Alexandria and become a devotee of the Egyptian goddess, Isis. Naturally, Clemens felt special gratitude to this goddess (who, though Egyptian in origin, was a favorite among the Roman slave-classes) for his luck in life.

fīnis

And so to the dénouement. On reaching home, Clemens finds the house
largely in ruins, and Caecilius dying, trapped under a fallen wall.
Caecilius persuades Clemens to flee for his life by suggesting that
Quintus may have survived, and that, if so, Clemens must find him.
Having entrusted his signet ring to Clemens for Quintus, Caecilius dies.
Clemens departs sadly, but Cerberus will not leave his master's body,
and remains in the house.

We do not actually know how the historical Caecilius died, but it is
not impossible (though, on chronological grounds, the balance of
probability is against it) that he was, as in the story "fīnis," a victim of
the A.D. 79 eruption. Make sure that the students notice the significance
of the ring (line 21). It symbolizes Quintus' new role as head of the
familia or its survivors. Some students, remembering the story about the
merchant who stamped a false agreement with his seal ring
("Hermogenēs," in Stage 4), will interpret the bequeathal as somewhat
ominous. Perhaps it is since later, in Unit 3, Quintus will barely escape
from Britain with his life.

Thus ends the narrative of Unit 1. After this melodramatic finale,
students may feel a bit of anti-climax. Some stalwart types will want to
discuss the fate of Caecilius' beloved wife Metella or of his dog Cerberus;
other more tender-hearted students will let these two quietly pass under
the ash-cover, not without tears. All students will have to wait a while
for the reappearance of Quintus and Clemens, as there is no sign of them
in Stage 13 of Unit 2. They will not have long to wait, however; Quintus
reappears in Stage 14; Clemens, soon afterwards—this time in new,
distant parts of the Roman Empire: Britain and Egypt, respectively.
Perhaps you will want to keep students guessing whether Quintus and
Clemens will reappear or not.

Language Note

After students have studied the language note, you might go on to drill
orally (asking for translations) Latin examples that contain the new
personal endings. Initially—or, with younger students, solely—you
should choose examples of the 1st and 2nd persons, singular and plural,
imperfect and perfect, from the stories in Stage 12 (e.g. *īnspiciēbāmus* or
audīvimus). If necessary, at first, mark the persons by adding pronouns
(e.g. *nōs īnspiciēbāmus*) but eventually omit them. Later, you might—with
older students, you should—drill additional examples formulated from
the verbs in the checklists, grouping examples within the several
conjugations to inculcate awareness of these. A catalogued list of
checklist verbs, Stages 1–9, was provided in the commentary on the first

language note, Stage 10, of this Manual (p. 85 above). Additional verbs, from the checklists of Stages 10–12, may be organized as follows:

1st	2nd	3rd
exclāmāre (10)	complēre (12)	āmittere (12)
invītāre (11)	favēre (11)	crēdere (11)
nūntiāre (10)	iacēre (12)	incidere (12)
servāre (10)	placēre (11)	legere (11)
verberāre (11)	tacēre (10)	mittere (12)
	timēre (12)	prōmittere (11)
		rapere (11)

3rd "-iō"	4th
accipere (10)	convenīre (11)
capere (10)	custōdīre (12)
fugere (12)	invenīre (10)
	sentīre (12)

Do not ask students to identify the conjugation of given verb-forms by number. It is enough for now that they should be able to handle the various forms within the categories that *you provide* by grouping drill-forms within the various conjugations.

Drills

There are no drills printed in Stage 12 of the students' textbook. Continue working in class or assigning as homework the remaining paragraphs of the Review Grammar part of the Language Information Section (pp. 202–12 of the students' textbook).

The Background Material

The story of the final catastrophe at Pompeii and the gradual rediscovery of it has been told in many places. You might supplement the information in the students' textbook with material from Brion 25–41, Maiuri, Wheeler, Paoli 135–37, or Marx 1–30. But the best description of the events themselves was written by Pliny the Younger. One or both of his letters should be read in translation to the class (*Letters*, VI.16 and 20). A paperbound, modern translation is available from Penguin Books; also in the Cambridge School Classics Project, The Roman World Foundation Course Booklet *Three Letters from Pliny*.

Students are sometimes surprised at the fate of Pompeii, given the distance of the town from Mount Vesuvius. The effect of the strength and direction of the wind during the eruption may need to be explained, with the help of the photograph of the 1944 eruption of Vesuvius shown on p. 198 and the map printed on p. 197 of the students' textbook. Marx

148–88 draws exact analogies between the eruption of Vesuvius and those of New World volcanoes like Mt. Pelée on the Caribbean island of Martinique, and Mt. St. Helens, in the state of Washington, United States. Mt. Pelée, like Vesuvius, destroyed good-sized towns—St. Pierre (A.D. 1902) and Pompeii (A.D. 79) respectively— both of which, being downwind from the volcano, were engulfed in a *nūbēs mīrābilis*. More recently, Mt. St. Helens erupted on 18 May 1980 and has continued erupting periodically since then. Splendid (or horrible, depending on one's proximity to the mountain) photographs of the *nūbēs* that accompanied that eruption may be found in *National Geographic Magazine*, January 1981, especially on fold-out pages 3–6. On p. 32 of the same issue is described one Harry Truman (not the American President), who, keeping a lodge on St. Helens and, refusing to abandon it, died inside, just as the equally stubborn Caecilius died (in our story) inside his villa at Pompeii.

You might also discuss the different fate of Herculaneum, which was not downwind, and was overwhelmed not by ash, but by a flow of mud and lava which then solidified to rock. Dramatic pictures of finds from recent excavations at Herculaneum have been published in *National Geographic Magazine*, May 1984 (cf. photograph on p. 196 of students' textbook).

Suggestions for Discussion

1 Discuss with the class the evidence of the suddenness of the end of Pompeii. How do we know, apart from the fact of the eruption, that the city did not simply fade out of existence gradually?
2 Discuss some of the difficulties that archaeologists face as they excavate the site of Pompeii. "Why has excavation taken so long—is, in fact, still in process?"

Words and Phrases Checklist

You might draw students' attention to the absence of a long mark over the first vowel in *fugit*, "runs away, flees." The equivalent perfect form would be *fūgit*, "ran away, fled." Remind students of analogously formed perfects: *agit/ēgit* (checklist, Stage 4), *emit/ēmit* (Stage 6), *capit/cēpit* (Stage 10), *facit/fēcit* (Stage 7), *legit/lēgit* (Stage 11), *venit/vēnit* (Stage 5), and now *fugit/fūgit* (Stage 12).

Suggestions for Further Work

1 Junior high school students enjoy drawing individual scenes or murals depicting the scene in Pompeian streets or in the forum during the eruption.

2 Ask high school students to write a news report describing the last day of Pompeii. Some students may prefer to tape-record their report "live" from Pompeii, complete with appropriately horrific sound effects.

3 Ask university students to write research papers, comparing the catastrophes at Pompeii, St. Pierre, and southwestern Washington state. Have them consult the *Reader's Guide to Periodical Literature, c.* 1902, for St. Pierre, and *c.* 1980, for St. Helens, to find contemporaneous accounts; then compare these with Pliny's eye-witness accounts in *Letters* VI.16 and 20, Penguin translation.

4 Divide the class into several groups. Ask each group to extemporize an episode from the eruption (not necessarily involving the family of Caecilius). Each group then performs its episode before the rest of the class. (Note: only the scenario need be written; actors may make up their lines as necessity or inspiration guides them.)

5 Show a videotape of the National Geographic Special TV Program, 1987: *Shadow of Vesuvius*. The documentary footage of the 1944 eruption of Mt. Vesuvius is particularly vivid, as well as an anthropologist's description of how life histories can be deduced from the appearance of the Roman bones found on the ancient beach at Herculaneum.

6 Set individual or group projects on topics relating to Unit 1 as a whole. Encourage students to choose their own topic and to find their own reference books. Possible topics might be the life of women; slave, freed, and free; travel and communications in the Roman Empire; Roman law; Roman coins and money; Roman religion and mythology; Pompeian influence on French furniture of Louis Seize, Directoire, and Empire styles; Edward Bulwer-Lytton's novel, *The Last Days of Pompeii* (1834); J. Paul Getty Museum, Malibu, California (built in the shape of the Villa dei Papiri, a large villa outside Herculaneum, overlooking the Bay of Naples and shown on p. 165 of the students' textbook); the *Pompeii AD 79* Exhibition that toured North America's major museums in 1979–81.

The Language Information Section

The Language Information Section consists of two parts: "Review Grammar" and "Complete Vocabulary." Following this section are a Guide to Characters and Places," "Index of Cultural Topics," "Index of Grammatical Topics," a "Time Chart," and a "Reference Grammar."

PART ONE: Review Grammar

This part serves two purposes. It provides students with a reference guide when they are completing drills as homework, preparing translations during study halls or at home or, during the later stages of Unit 1, reviewing and integrating inflections and grammar. Because this is retrospective in tone, it is not very suitable for introducing students to new points.

This collects and amplifies various grammatical points that have been introduced and described in several previous stages, e.g. the nominative, accusative and dative cases of the noun; the singular and plural personal endings of the verb; and the present, imperfect and perfect tenses. It also comments on certain grammatical points that have come to light in the students' readings, without being discussed in any of the language notes within the stages, e.g. the clauses headed by *postquam* and *quod*. The subsections on nouns and verbs repeat and schematize every inflection that appears in the language notes within the separate stages. These inflections, schematized into paradigms, will reappear in the corresponding Language Information Sections of subsequent Units—thus providing a complete overview of noun and verb systems in Latin. The sub-sections on word order and syntax are more selective; they do not necessarily review the word patterns that are picked out in the language notes within the stages. Thus the syntactic information in the section becomes less repetitive and space is reserved for the more important features.

The drills incorporated into the "Review Grammar" part are usually somewhat harder than those in the individual stages. They are devised primarily for oral drill in class, to be used at whatever point in Unit 1 you believe the students can most usefully, confidently, and successfully complete them. You should therefore, allow ample time to intervene between study of a grammatical point in the language note of an individual stage and the review of that same point in the drills of the Language Information Sections. Otherwise, students will not have a chance to become familiar with the inflection or grammatical point through their reading.

Work in the Language Information Section might begin when students reach approximately Stage 10, and continue thereafter *pari passu* with the closing stages of Unit 1. You might postpone one or two of the drills in the section until after students have finished Unit 1 or even until after they have started Unit 2. If you decide to drill the entire section after Stage 12 and before Stage 13 you may severely disrupt the mental digestive processes of your students. Much later, when students are well along in Unit 2, you might want to repeat, for oral translation by the students, some of the forms in the Unit 1 Language Information Section, especially the sentences in the "Word Order" sub-section, as a purely aural exercise in which students do not have the Latin in front of them, but listen to it being read (or repeated from memory) by you.

The following comments are concerned with the individual sub-sections of the Language Information Section:

Nouns (pp. 202–203). When drilling the singular-to-plural and plural-to-singular transformations, remind students of the meaning of the complete sentence in which particular nouns are singled out for change. Here, as always in drills, emphasize the connection between *form* and *function* of a particular case. Otherwise, students learn spelling but not usage of nouns. To insure in students overall comprehension as well as attention to spelling, read out the entire sentence and ask a volunteer to translate it, both before and after a student has changed the number of the boldly printed Latin noun. Sometimes, however, omit such translations in order to keep the pace from lagging.

Verbs (pp. 204–206). The paradigms of the present tense of the four conjugations (including the subgroup of the third conjugation, known as the "-iō" verbs) are printed for students to review rather than to memorize and recite as itemized wholes. In learning Latin, as in learning any language, the important thing is that students should understand the meaning or use of inflections when they meet them in a passage of continuous Latin. Learning paradigms or discontinuous lists may sometimes contribute little or nothing to skill in comprehension. Students who are able to recite paradigms may be unable to apply their knowledge of paradigms to their reading. Conversely, students may be able to recognize inflections like -*s*, -*mus*, -*nt* etc. in their reading, and translate them accurately, solely through experience and understanding, without having formally memorized them in systematized lists.

The verb inflections listed on p. 204 of the section (and drilled in the accompanying integration exercises) are present tense and the 3rd person singular and plural of the imperfect and perfect tenses. Students will have had considerable practice reading examples of these during the final stages of Unit 1. The 1st and 2nd persons of the imperfect and perfect are not presented until Stage 12, where they are described in an accompanying language note that students may consult while they are reading that stage. The Language Information Section of Unit 2 presents all three tenses (present, imperfect, and perfect) with all three persons and both numbers. While students are studying Unit 2, they should learn to discriminate accurately among all forms of these tenses. In Unit 1, however, students should concentrate on learning to understand forms of the present tense and of the 3rd person imperfect and perfect.

At this point in their progress, students should not be forced to learn the differences in the present tense among the conjugations, since those are less important than their similarities. Direct the students' attention to the -*ō*, -*s*, -*t*, -*mus*, -*tis*, and -*nt* (the -*t* and -*nt* endings are common to the 3rd person imperfect and perfect forms too). These endings are the same in the present tense of all four conjugations. To comprehend meanings, students do not need to differentiate among the vowels that characterize the conjugations and may precede the endings listed above. Discrimination among the conjugations is a matter of correct spelling, comes with experience and time, and is crucial basically to correct writing, not reading, of Latin.

Ways of Forming the Perfect Tense (pp. 207–209). Have students study this subsection in order to fix in their minds the general difference between regular perfects with -*v*- or -*u*- and irregular perfects with a variety of inflections which at this point should simply be recognized as perfect. When students are working from Latin to English (rather than from English to Latin) they do not need to know ahead of time how each verb forms its perfect.

Word Order (pp. 210–11). If students (usually the younger ones) have difficulty understanding sentences without subjects specified separately (e.g. *poētam audīvit* or *amīcum salūtās*), prompt them with analogous sentences that specify the subject separately (e.g. *mercātor poētam audīvit* or *tū amīcum salūtās*). Do not attempt an analysis into accusative + verb and unexpressed nominative. A student who cannot understand the sentence is unlikely to understand an abstract analysis. The proper time for abstract analysis is after further practice with additional Latin examples. When students are consistently getting the drill-examples right, the analysis is more likely to make sense to them.

Longer Sentences with "postquam" and "quod" (p. 212). The sentence-examples in paragraph 3 illustrate a piece-by-piece approach to the reading of complex sentences which you will want to imitate many times in the Units to come when students are having difficulty.

PART TWO: Complete Vocabulary

This section is a cumulated vocabulary for the entire Unit. Its format and content are explained in notes on pp. 213–14 of the students' textbook. Go through these notes with the class. Remember that students do not meet perfect-tense forms (discussed in notes 4–6) until Stage 6. Use the drill-examples in the notes to make sure that students understand them.

Some classes, in our experience, have become over-dependent on the Unit's cumulated vocabulary. The problem usually originates in the students' forming early a habit that their teacher could and should have discouraged. You can deter students from wearing out the cumulated vocabulary section by doing as much *first* reading as possible in class, where students can consult the collective memory of the class (or of the group, if they are working in groups) before they turn to the back of the Language Information Section. You should not (unless students are very able) assign as first readings, translations to be prepared at home, where students can easily fall into the habit of thumbing the vocabulary at the back. Rather, encourage students to work out together large amounts of initial translation in class, depending, for speed of comprehension, on each other's collective memory. Although not all students remember all words, all together will remember most of them, and thereby set a good example for the students who remember few. Finally, strengthen students' memories by drilling words and inflections, asking for translations of the most common words, both in context and, separately, out of context. (These words are readily found in the checklists and the Cumulated List of Checklist Words in Appendix A of this Manual, pp. 114–16 below.)

Here is a sample vocabulary drill for some of the words in the checklist of Stage 12: "If *āmīsit* means 'he lost', what would *āmittēbat* mean? If *āmittēbat* means 'he was losing', what would *āmittit* mean? If *fundum āmīsit* means 'he lost his farm', what would *ē fundō fūgit* mean? If *ē fundō fūgit* means 'he fled from the farm', what would *fundum āmīsit* mean? If *cinis incidit* means 'the ash fell', what would *nūbēs mīrābilis incidit* mean? *cinis incidit* can also mean 'the ash falls'; give two meanings for *flamma incidit*. If *in terrā iacet* means 'he is lying on the ground', what would *iacet in templō* (Be careful!) mean? What does *nūbem sēnsit* mean? What does *flammam sēnsit* mean? What does *flammam paene sēnsit* mean? What does *epistulam mīsit* mean?"

Write out similar drills for each of the stage checklists and keep them ready at hand. Such drills are excellent pace-changers, and they are effective even if only two or three minutes of the class-period remain for them. Should only a minute remain before the bell rings, try a fast "lightning" drill: cite roots or stems only, asking students to call out the dictionary meanings. For example: *errā-* (Answer: wander), *mitte-* (send), *sentī-* (feel), *terra* (ground), *fort-* (strong), *mont-* (mountain), *nūb-* (cloud), *dēns-* (thick), *ciner-* (ash), and so forth. To teach students to comprehend Latin while they read it, there is perhaps no better drill than this "lightning" kind that provides practice in understanding the basic meanings of words.

Diagnostic Tests

The tests below are designed, not to measure achievement, but to diagnose students' progress; to determine, at periodic intervals, the degree to which students

have understood recent material;
have integrated less recent material into their understanding;
need review of grammar;
need drill in basic vocabulary.

The tests are not "norm-referenced," i.e. designed to distinguish sharply between more- and less-able students to provide a good grade-curve. From the teacher's viewpoint, the total number of points earned by each student is less important than his/her performance in specific sections (see the comments following Test 3 below). Resist, however, the impulse to review intensively areas in which students show themselves, on these diagnostic tests, to be weak. More properly, incorporate such review into your lesson plans over a span of weeks.

In the tests, the words and phrases in heavy type are either new to students or have appeared infrequently in the stages. You might provide meanings for these words, since most students are unlikely to recognize words they have seen only once or twice previously.

When correcting the tests, keep the following points in mind:

1 Any English translation that faithfully reflects the meaning of the Latin is acceptable. Do not insist on structural equivalence.
2 Do not take off an excessive number of points if students mistake the meaning or inflection of words with which they have not long been familiar.
3 Students will probably have most difficulty with sentences that show a strong contrast with English structure (e.g. sentences with subject omitted).

The majority of students should find these tests well within their ability. Where they have difficulty, refer them back to sentences that illustrate the point causing them difficulty (model sentences are often suitable for this purpose), and then, if necessary, make up further examples for the students to translate.

Test 1

To be given to pupils after Stage 4 has been completed.

ad carcerem

    iūdex Hermogenem **convincit.**
    "ego Hermogenem **ad carcerem mittō**," inquit iūdex.
    "ego sum **innocēns**," clāmat Hermogenēs.
    "**immō**, tū es mercātor **scelestus**!" respondet iūdex, "tū **multam**
pecūniam dēbēs."   5
    servus mercātōrem scelestum ē basilicā **trahit.** servus mercātōrem
ad carcerem dūcit et iānuam **pulsat. custōs** iānuam **aperit.** custōs
est Grōma. Grōma mercātōrem **statim agnōscit.** Grōma rīdet.
    "Hermogenēs est amīcus **veterrimus**," inquit Grōma.
    "Hermogenēs vīllam nōn habet. Hermogenēs in carcere **habitat**!"   10
    servus rīdet. sed Hermogenēs nōn rīdet. Hermogenēs Grōmam
vituperat. Grōma est īrātus. Grōma mercātōrem ad carcerem
trahit.
    "**cella tua** est **parāta**," inquit Grōma.

Test 2

To be given at the end of Stage 8.

vīlla scelesta

    in urbe erat vīlla pulchra. vīlla tamen erat **vacua**, quod umbra
ibi habitābāt. omnēs **cīvēs** umbram valdē timēbant.
    Athēnodōrus ad urbem vēnit et **dē umbrā** audīvit. Athēnodōrus
tamen umbrās nōn timēbat, quod erat **philosophus**. vīllam igitur
ēmit.   5
    postquam **nox** vēnit, Athēnodōrus in ātriō sedēbat. subitō
philosophus **fragōrem** audīvit. **respexit** et umbram **horribilem**
vīdit. umbra erat senex et multās **catēnās gerēbat.** umbra,
postquam **ingemuit**, ad hortum **lentē** ambulābat. Athēnodōrus
quoque ad hortum ambulāvit. postquam Athēnodōrus hortum   10
intrāvit, umbra subitō **ēvānuit.**
    tum Athēnodōrus servōs vocāvit. servī **palās** portāvērunt et
hortum intrāvērunt. servī, postquam in hortō **fōdērunt, hominem**
mortuum **invēnērunt.**
    Athēnodōrus hominem **rītē sepelīvit**, quod philosophus erat   15
benignus. Athēnodōrus umbram **numquam** iterum vīdit.

Test 3

To be given during or at the end of Stage 12.

Caecilius et Phormiō

ōlim mercātor diem nātālem celebrābat. mercātor Caecilium ad
cēnam invītāvit. Caecilius cum servō ad vīllam contendit, ubi
mercātor habitābat. servus erat Phormiō. Caecilius, postquam
vīllam intrāvit, multōs amīcōs vīdit. cēna amīcōs valdē dēlectāvit.
omnēs multum vīnum bibēbant et multās fābulās nārrābant.   5
tandem ē vīllā discessērunt. Caecilius et Phormiō quoque
discessērunt. viae erant **dēsertae**, quod omnēs Pompēiānī
dormiēbant.

trēs fūrēs tamen per viās **errābant**. fūrēs, postquam Caecilium
cōnspexērunt, dīxērunt,   10
"ecce! Caecilius adest. Caecilius est argentārius et multam
pecūniam habet."
fūrēs Caecilium ferōciter pulsābant. Caecilium ad **terram**
dēiēcērunt. Phormiō tamen ad fūrēs **sē praecipitāvit** et omnēs
superāvit. Caecilius postquam **convaluit**, Phormiōnem **līberāvit**.   15
Caecilius Phormiōnī pecūniam dedit, quod fidēlis erat.

These tests help you diagnose the student's progress at several points.
For example, Test 3 might yield the following diagnosis:

Possible problems with meanings

ubi (line 2), *valdē* (4), *dēlectāre* (4), *discēdere* (6), *pulsāre* (13), *fidēlis* (16).

Possible problems with inflection of noun

viae (7).

Possible problems with inflections of verbs

imperfect, e.g. *celebrābat* (1) and (for older students, to whom the
inceptive force of the imperfect was mentioned) *pulsābant* (13).

Possible problems with sentence structure

(a) Single subject of two verbs:
     omnēs multum vīnum bibēbant ... nārrābant (4).
     Caecilius est argentārius et ... habet (11–12).
     Phormiō tamen ad fūrēs ... omnēs superāvit (14–15).

(b) Subject of intransitive verb not expressed:
tandem ē vīllā discessērunt (6).

(c) Subject of transitive verb not expressed:
Caecilium ad terram dēiēcērunt (13–14).

Possible problems with "postquam" -clauses

Caecilius, postquam vīllam intrāvit, multōs amīcōs vīdit (3–4).
fūrēs, postquam Caecilium cōnspexērunt, dīxērunt (9–10).
Caecilius postquam convaluit, ... līberāvit (15).

Are any students getting the sentence wrong by treating *postquam* as an adverb?.

Are any students having difficulty with the accusative of the verb in the *postquam*-clause (e.g. translating "Caecilius was seen" for *Caecilium cōnspexērunt*)?

Are some of the better students preferring "After Caecilius recovered ..." to "Caecilius, after he recovered, ..."?

Are some students relying on the comma before a subordinate clause to identify it? (The first two examples have one; the third one doesn't.)

Appendix A: Cumulated List of Checklist Words

The number in brackets refers to the stage in which the word appears in the checklist.

a
abesse (6)
abīre (10)
accipere (10)
ad (3)
adesse (5)
agere (4)
agitāre (8)
agnōscere (9)
agricola (5)
ambulāre (5)
amīcus (2)
āmittere (12)
ancilla (2)
ānulus (4)
ātrium (1)
audīre (5)
avārus (6)

b
bibere (3)

c
callidus (10)
canis (1)
capere (10)
celebrāre (9)
celeriter (9)
cēna (2)
cēnāre (7)
centuriō (7)
cēra (4)
cibus (2)
cinis (12)
circumspectāre (3)

cīvis (9)
clāmāre (3)
clāmor (5)
complēre (12)
cōnspicere (7)
cōnsūmere (8)
contendere (5)
contentus (10)
convenīre (11)
coquere (4)
coquus (1)
crēdere (11)
cubiculum (6)
cum (= with) (7)
cupere (9)
cūr? (4)
currere (5)
custōdīre (12)

d
dare (9)
dē (= about) (11)
dēnsus (12)
diēs (9)
diēs nātālis (9)
dominus (2)
dormīre (2)
dūcere (8)
duo (12)

e
ē (4)
ecce! (3)
ego (4)

ēheu! (4)
emere (6)
ēmittere (9)
epistula (12)
esse (1)
et (3)
euge! (5)
eum (8)
exclāmāre (10)
exercēre (9)
exīre (3)
exspectāre (3)

f
fābula (5)
fābulam agere (5)
facere (7)
facile (8)
favēre (11)
fēmina (5)
ferōciter (6)
ferōx (8)
ferre (9)
festīnāre (6)
filius (1)
flamma (12)
fortis (6)
fortiter (12)
forum (3)
frāter (10)
frūstrā (12)
fugere (12)
fundus (12)
fūr (6)

g
gēns (11)
gladius (8)
gustāre (2)

h
habēre (4)
habitāre (8)
hercle! (10)
heri (7)
hic (8)
hodiē (5)
homō (9)
hortus (1)
hospes (9)

i
iacēre (12)
iam (12)
iānua (3)
igitur (12)
ignāvus (8)
ille (9)
imperium (10)
in (1)
incidere (12)
incitāre (8)
īnfāns (6)
ingēns (7)
inimīcus (10)
inquit (4)
īnspicere (9)
intellegere (7)
intentē (6)
intrāre (2)
invenīre (10)
invītāre (11)
īrātus (3)
īre (10)
iterum (9)
iūdex (4)
iuvenis (5)

l
labōrāre (1)
lacrimāre (7)
laetus (2)
laudāre (2)
legere (11)
leō (3)
liber (10)
līberālis (11)
lībertus (6)

m
magnus (3)
manēre (9)
māter (1)
medius (9)
mendāx (4)
mēnsa (2)
mercātor (2)
meus (5)
minimē! (11)
mīrābilis (12)
mittere (12)
mōns (12)
mortuus (7)
mox (9)
multī (5)
multus (5)
mūrus (11)

n
nārrāre (7)
nāvis (3)
necāre (7)
negōtium agere (4)
nihil (7)
nōn (3)
nōs (10)
noster (11)
nōtus (9)
nūbēs (12)
nunc (11)
nūntiāre (10)
nūntius (8)

o
offere (9)
ōlim (6)
omnis (7)
optimē (12)
optimus (5)
ostendere (9)

p
paene (12)
parāre (7)
parvus (6)
pater (1)
paulīsper (9)
pāx (10)
pecūnia (4)
per (6)
perterritus (4)
pēs (8)
pestis (7)
petere (5)
placēre (11)
plaudere (5)
pōculum (7)
poēta (4)
porta (8)
portāre (3)
portus (10)
post (9)
postquam (6)
postulāre (8)
prīmus (11)
prōcēdere (7)
prōmittere (11)
prope (7)
puella (5)
puer (8)
pugna (11)
pugnāre (8)
pulcher (7)
pulsāre (6)

q
quaerere (4)

quam (= than) (10)
quis? (4)
quod (= because) (6)
quoque (2)

r
rapere (11)
recumbere (8)
reddere (4)
rēs (6)
respondēre (3)
revenīre (9)
rīdēre (3)
rogāre (7)

s
saepe (8)
salūtāre (2)
salvē! (3)
sanguis (8)
satis (4)
scrībere (6)
secundus (11)
sed (4)
sedēre (1)
semper (10)
senātor (11)
senex (5)
sententia (10)
sentīre (12)

servāre (10)
servus (1)
signum (4)
silva (8)
sollicitus (11)
sōlus (10)
spectāculum (8)
spectāre (5)
stāre (5)
statim (8)
stultus (11)
subitō (6)
superāre (6)
surgere (3)
suus (9)

t
taberna (3)
tacēre (10)
tacitē (7)
tamen (7)
tandem (12)
templum (12)
terra (12)
terrēre (7)
tertius (11)
timēre (12)
tōtus (8)
trādere (9)
trēs (12)

tū (4)
tuba (8)
tum (6)
turba (5)
tuus (6)

u
ubi (= where) (5)
umbra (7)
ūnus (12)
urbs (5)
ūtilis (11)
uxor (10)

v
valdē (7)
valē! (11)
vehementer (10)
vēnātiō (8)
vēndere (4)
venīre (5)
verberāre (11)
via (1)
vidēre (3)
vīlla (3)
vīnum (3)
vir (11)
vituperāre (6)
vocāre (4)
vōs (10)

Appendix B: Summary of Changes from the North American Second Edition

General

The principles on which the North American Second Edition was designed remain the same (see "Objectives of the Course," pp. 5–6 above). The North American Third Edition is compatible with the North American Second Edition. In the Third Edition, however, the students' textbook has been written in American English throughout, with punctuation, spelling, and analogies in the American style; many new photographs, including color ones, have been added; slight (mostly cosmetic) changes have been made to some of the line drawings.

Particular

Changes from the North American Second Edition of Unit I include the following:

1 Unit I has been renumbered with an Arabic numeral as Unit 1 to avoid confusion between the name of the textbook and "Latin I," the traditional name for first-year high-school Latin, the curriculum of which normally requires both Units 1 and 2 (formerly Units I and IIA/IIB) of the *Cambridge Latin Course*.

2 The students' material has been bound with the former Language Information pamphlet into a single hardbound volume. There have been added an Index of Cultural Topics (formerly in the Unit I Teacher's Manual, p. 114), a new Index of Grammatical Topics, a new Time Chart, and a new Reference Grammar printed conveniently on the back endpaper.

3 The contents of the former Language Information pamphlet have been retitled as the Language Information Section. Part One of the Language Information Section has been renamed "Review Grammar"; Part Two, "Complete Vocabulary." The "Guide to Characters and Places" appears, as previously, immediately after the cumulated vocabulary.

4 Latin Names and Proper Adjectives are now glossed in sections separate from the other Latin words in the running vocabularies.

5 A new sub-section, entitled "Metella," has been added to the background material in Stage 1.

6 Slightly new wording has been introduced into lines 8–9 of the story, "fābula mīrābilis" in Stage 7 (p. 102) so as to allow the centurion to change into a werewolf under the traditional full moon (see Petronius, *Satyricon* 62.3: *luna lucebat tamquam meridie*).

7 A new drill, called Word Search, follows the Words and Phrases Checklist in every Stage. This drill uses Latin words in the preceding checklist as clues for matching definitions with the correct English words.

8 The Teacher's Manual has been streamlined to make it more accessible. New charts outlining Narrative Points, Grammatical Points, and Sentence Patterns have been introduced into the beginning of each of the Stage Commentaries. The Bibliography has been updated. As there is now a Word Search drill in every Stage the lists of derivatives have been omitted.

Bibliography

Books marked with an asterisk (*) are suitable for use by junior high or high school students; other books, by college or university students (or high school students under the teacher's guidance). Included are some recommended books which, though out of print (O.P.), may sometimes be found in libraries or second-hand bookstores.

Unless stated otherwise, publishers cited are British. But if a book printed in Great Britain is or was available from a North American distributor, the name of the latter—should it differ from that of the British publisher—is listed. If in print, British books without North American distributors may be ordered from Heffers Bookstore, 10 Trinity Street, Cambridge CB2 3NG, ENGLAND. To establish a personal account (and obtain instructions for ordering), request an application blank from Heffers, c/o Customers' Accounts Department, P.O. Box 33, Cambridge CB2 1TX, ENGLAND.

For up-to-date listings of audio-visual materials, consult the frequent listings in *Classical World*: the most recent is J. C. Traupman, "1987 Survey of Audio-Visual Materials in the Classics" *Classical World* Vol. 80, 1987, pp. 245–309.

For a current list of supplementary materials and examinations available specifically for users of the *Cambridge Latin Course*, write to William D. Gleason, Director, Resource Center, North American Cambridge Classics Project (NACCP), Box 932, Amherst, MA 01004–0932, U.S.A.

Pompeii and Herculaneum

Andrews, I. *Pompeii (Cambridge University Press 1980; Minneapolis, MN: Lerner Publications).

Brion, M. *Pompeii and Herculaneum: The Glory and the Grief* (Paul Elek 1977, O.P.).

Connolly, P. *Pompeii (MacDonald 1979). Highly recommended.

de Franciscis, A. *Pompeii (Interdipress, Via Galileo Ferraris 132, Naples). Guide in full color; available at the site.

The Buried Cities (Orbis Publishing 1979).

Deiss, J. J. *Herculaneum* (Souvenir Press 1968, O.P.).

The Town of Hercules (Evans Brothers 1976).

Grant, M. *Cities of Vesuvius* (Weidenfeld and Nicolson 1971, O.P.; Penguin 1976, O.P.).

The Art and Life of Pompeii and Herculaneum (New York: Newsweek 1979, O.P.).

History Today, April 1964, "The Small Gardens of Pompeii."

Hollinghurst, H. (ed.). *Greeks and Romans* (Heinemann 1974, O.P.). Contains useful material on Pompeii.

Kraus, T. *Pompeii and Herculaneum: The Living Cities of the Dead* (New York: Harry N. Abrams 1975, O.P.).

Maiuri, A. *Guide to Pompeii* (Libreria dello Stato, 14th edn 1974; Piazza G. Verdi 10, Rome).

National Geographic Magazine, January 1981, "Eruption of Mount St. Helens." Contains photographs of a North American eruption similar to that of Vesuvius.

May 1984, "The Dead Do Tell Tales at Vesuvius." Contains photographs of Roman skeletons and a boat discovered on the beach at Herculaneum.

Pereira, A. *Naples, Pompeii and Southern Italy* (Batsford 1977, O.P.).

Pompeii AD 79 Catalogue (Imperial Tobacco Ltd. 1976, O.P.; Boston Museum of Fine Arts 1978, O.P.).

Princeton Encyclopedia of Classical Sites (Princeton University Press 1976). See the entry under "Pompeii."

Santini, L. *Pompeii, the Excavations* (Fotorapidacolor Terni, Italy). Color guide.

Naples and Surroundings (Fotorapidacolor Terni, Italy). Color guide. Both guides by Santini are available at the site.

Seaford, R. *Pompeii* (Thames and Hudson 1979; New York: W. W. Norton, 1979, O.P.).

Tanzer, H. H. *The Common People of Pompeii* (Baltimore: Johns Hopkins Press 1939, O.P.).

Trevelyan, R. *The Shadow of Vesuvius* (Folio Society and Michael Joseph 1976, O.P.).

Unstead, R. J. *Living in Pompeii* (Black 1976).

Wheeler, Sir Mortimer. *Introduction to Pompeii and Herculaneum* (Spring Books 1966, O.P.).

Will, E. L. "Women in Pompeii" *Archaeology* (September/October 1979), pp. 34–43.

Historical Novels

Dillon, E. *The Shadow of Vesuvius* (Faber 1978; New York: Elsevier/Nelson Books 1978, O.P.).

Lloyd, A. *The Taras Report on the Last Days of Pompeii* (Souvenir Press 1977; Portland, OR: International Specialized Book Services 1977).

Wilson, B. K. *Beloved of the Gods* (Constable 1965, O.P.).

The Tablets of Caecilius

The complete collection is in *Corpus Inscriptionum Latinarum (C.I.L.)* IV,
　　Supplement Part I. Selections may be found in the following:
Andreau, Jean. *Les Affairs de Monsieur Jucundus* (Ecole Francaise de
　　Rome, 1974). Contains text of 31 tablets.
Marx, Walter H. *Claimed by Vesuvius* (The Independent School Press, 2nd
　　edn 1979, distributed by White Plains, NY: Longman Group USA).
　　Contains text of 13 tablets.

General

Allen, W. S. *Vox Latina* (Cambridge University Press, 2nd edn 1978).
Apicius. *The Roman Cookery Book*, trs. B. Flower and E. Rosenbaum
　　(Harrap 1974).
Balsdon, J. P. V. D. *Life and Leisure in Ancient Rome* (Bodley Head 1969,
　　O.P.).
　Roman Women (Barnes & Noble Books (pbd) 1983, distributed by NY:
　　Harper and Row).
Barrow, R. *Greek and Roman Education* (Macmillan 1976).
Bonner, S. F. *Education in Ancient Rome* (Methuen 1977; Berkeley, CA:
　　University of California Press (pbd) 1977).
Cambridge School Classics Project *How the Greeks and Romans Made Cloth*
　　(Book 2 of Cambridge Classical Studies 13–16: Cambridge
　　University Press 1984).
Carcopino, J. *Daily Life in Ancient Rome* (New Haven, CT: Yale
　　University Press 1940).
Cowell, F. R. *Everyday Life in Ancient Rome* (Batsford 1961, O.P.; Carousel
　　Books 1975, O.P.).
Cullum, A. *Greek Tears and Roman Laughter* (New York: Citation 1970,
　　O.P.).
D'Arms, J. H. *Commerce and Social Standing in Ancient Rome* (Cambridge,
　　MA: Harvard University Press, 1981).
Dilke, O. A. W. *The Ancient Romans: How They Lived and Worked* (David
　　and Charles 1975, O.P.).
　The Roman Land Surveyors (David and Charles 1971).
Finley, M. I. *The Ancient Economy* (Chatto and Windus 1973, pbd 1975).
Grant, M. *Gladiators* (Weidenfeld and Nicolson 1967, O.P.; Penguin
　　1971, O.P.).
Hamey, L. A. and J. A. *The Roman Engineers* (Cambridge University
　　Press 1981; Minneapolis, MN: Lerner Publications).
Hodge, P. *Roman House* (Longman 1976).
　Roman Towns (Longman, rev. edn 1977).
　Roman Family Life (Longman 1974).

Aspects of Roman Life: Folder I (Longman 1977). Material supplementary to the above topics.

Hopkins, K. *Conquerors and Slaves* (Cambridge University Press 1978; pbd 1981).

Lefkowitz, M. R. and Fant, M. B. *Women's Life in Greece and Rome* (Baltimore, MD: Johns Hopkins University Press, rev. edn (pbd) 1982).

Lewis, N. and Reinhold, M. *Roman Civilization: A Sourcebook*. I *The Republic*; II *The Empire* (New York: Harper and Row 1966; Harper Torchbooks).

McLeish, K. *Food and Drink* (Greek and Roman Topics Series: Winchester, MA; Allen and Unwin (pbd) 1978).

Marrou, H. I. *A History of Education in Antiquity* (Madison, WI: University of Wisconsin Press (pbd) 1982).

Paoli, U. E. *Rome, its People, Life and Customs* (Longman 1963, O.P.).